Family, Friends & Strangers

Family, Friends & Strangers

Every Christian's Guide to Counseling

Lowell D. Streiker

Abingdon Press

Nashville

Family, Friends, and Strangers
Every Christian's Guide to Counseling

This book is printed on acid-free paper.

Library of Congress Cataloging-in-Publication Data

STREIKER, LOWELL D.
    Family, friends, and strangers: every Christian's guide to counsel-
ing / Lowell D. Streiker
        p.   cm.
    ISBN 0-687-12715-7 (pbk.: alk. paper)
    1. Peer counseling in the church. 2. Counseling. I. Title.
BV4409.S86 1988   87-31827
253.5—dc19   CIP

Unless otherwise indicated Scripture quotations in this publication are from
the Revised Standard Version of the Bible, copyrighted 1946, 1952, © 1971,
1973 by the Division of Christian Education of the National Council of the
Churches of Christ in the U.S.A., and used by permission.

New Testament citations indicated LDS have been translated by the author
directly from the original Greek text.

The Beck scripture quotations are from *The New Testament in the Language of
Today* by William F. Beck. Copyright © 1963 by Concordia Publishing House.

MANUFACTURED BY THE PARTHENON PRESS
NASHVILLE, TENNESSEE, UNITED STATES OF AMERICA

To our grandson
Jonathan David

CONTENTS

Family, Friends & Strangers

INTRODUCTION

Do you want to make a difference in the lives of others?

Are you a caring person? Do you wish that you could make things better for those who are frightened or confused?

When your best friend is hurting, do you want to help? When your children need your advice (but do not know that they need it), would you like to be able to respond to them? Do you feel that even though you are a compassionate friend, you really could learn to be a more effective adviser? When those close to you are angry or anxious or depressed, do you wish you could be more helpful, more understanding, more caring?

Do you wish you knew what to say to someone who is going through a divorce or is grieving the death of a loved one or is mourning the passing of what has been and can never be again?

If your answer to these questions is yes, *Family, Friends, and Strangers* is intended as your guidebook. It is designed to help you answer one fundamental question, How can I as a Christian effectively and responsibly serve as counselor and adviser to my friends, loved ones, and neighbors? Or to state this in other words, "Given who I am as a child of God, how can

I make a difference in the lives of those with whom I am inextricably involved in my daily life?"

In this book, I am trying to convey to you what I have learned as a counselor who has a deep interest in theology and the Bible. In setting forth these lessons, I have avoided professional jargon and buzz words. Counseling, as the term is used in this book, is the natural expression of a relationship of trust and caring that the counselor has established with another person. The counselor may be a parent, grandparent, spouse, child, friend, neighbor, or co-worker of the person counseled. The person being counseled may be the parent, grandparent, spouse, child, friend, neighbor, or co-worker of the counselor. I have chosen the term "friend" instead of "client" or "subject" to refer to the person being counseled. My goal is to explain in simple, nontechnical terms how you may enhance your intuitive counseling abilities in order to respond compassionately and effectively to those in need. My goal is to teach you how to help others live more comfortably within their own skins, to rediscover their own sense of who they are and to whom they are responsible, and to find in their personal faith a renewed courage for responding to the challenges of their own lives.

Family, Friends, and Strangers is based on the real experiences of real people—on the lives of those whom I have known as friends or clients during my many years as crisis counselor, minister, teacher, and mental health administrator. The approach is extremely personal, that is, grounded in my experiences as a Christian who has been involved in the crises of several hundred families. Whenever possible, I have presented notes from actual stories or anecdotes from my own life. My purpose in telling these stories is not to show how successful I have been as a counselor. Being there for one's friend and being responsible is all that can be required of any counselor—whatever the result may be. For the most part, I have employed the case notes to provide graphic, concrete instances of such common problems as depression and anxiety or to relate valuable lessons that my friends and clients have taught me. (Names and circumstantial details have been changed to ensure the privacy of all involved.) To these lessons I have added my observations, relevant biblical passages, and step-by-step "how to do it" suggestions.

Family, Friends, and Strangers opens with a consideration of the theological basis for counseling; it then moves on to concrete suggestions on how to give advice, how to become an agent of personal transformation, how to respond to anger, depression, anxiety, marital discord. I have chosen to include my theological musings, to "begin with first things first," for two reasons, to emphasize (a) that your effectiveness as a counselor depends on your own spiritual well-being and that your perspective as a Christian is the foundation of any influence that you may have on the life of another and (b) that the lives and situations of the friends whom you counsel cannot be changed for the better unless there is also clarification on their part of what they believe and to whom they are ultimately responsible. I have tried to balance the sound professionalism that I have learned from my colleagues and mentors in the mental health profession with the spiritual convictions that are mine as a Christian and a student of religious experience.

What I want to say in this book is that both caring and skill are essential and inseparable if one is to be an agent of personal transformation; that a totally sentimental, nonjudgmental attitude of acceptance and understanding is never enough; that love without reason makes for disastrous counseling while insight without compassion is futile; and that Christian self-awareness and the willingness to share the deepest secrets of one's own identity are powerful factors in influencing others.

Every morning, I take a short walk in a small waterfront park near my home. This is my time for prayer and meditation. My prayers for the day invariably close with the Lord's Prayer (Matt. 6:9-15). As I silently repeat these few sentences, I observe, as though I were a witness to my own thinking process, how the words of the Lord's Prayer apply themselves to my concerns for the coming day. Thus anchored in who I am and to whom I belong, I return home, and the tranquilities and the anxieties, joys and sorrows, challenges and opportunities, certitudes and confusions, harmonies and noise of my life rush in to greet me. Just as the Lord's Prayer structures my day, so have I chosen it as the framework for *Family, Friends, and Strangers*.

PART I

THE COUNSELOR'S PERSPECTIVE

Our Father, who is in heaven,
Let your name be kept holy;
And let your kingdom come;
Let your will come about
just as it is in heaven, so
let it be on earth (Matt. 6:9-10 LDS).

And he came to Nazareth, where he had been brought up, and he entered according to his custom on the day of the sabbath into the synagogue, and he stood up to read. And a scroll of the prophet Isaiah was handed to him, and having opened the scroll he found the place where it was written: "The Spirit of the Lord is upon me, that is why he anointed me to evangelize the poor, he has sent me to proclaim release to captives, and sight to the blind, to set at liberty those who have been crushed, to proclaim the acceptable year of the Lord." And having closed the scroll, and returning it to the attendant he sat down, and the eyes of all in the synagogue were gazing at him. And he began to say to them, "Today this scripture has been fulfilled in your ears. . . . To be sure you will say to me this proverb: "Physician, cure yourself" (Luke 4:16-23 LDS).

CHAPTER 1

The Counselor's Perspective

Case Notes: Ted

A good friend during my years as a faculty member at a university in the northeast was a professor of classics whom we shall call Ted. Ted was warm, caring, entertaining, and spiritual. He was what I would term "a monster of love." No matter what he did, he did without reservation or hesitation. Unfortunately, many of his causes, loves, and commitments ended in disaster. Before I knew him, he had been a Catholic priest. In his zeal to help the church open its windows to the fresh air of reform, he had alienated his colleagues and superiors and had been sent into virtual exile as a chaplain at a boarding school in Europe. There he met an equally reform-minded nun. Exhilarated by visions of sharing their Vatican II–inspired faith and social conscience with the "secular city," they obtained dispensations from their respective vows and were married.

Ted's doctorate in classics and several scholarly articles that had been published during his time in the order enabled him to begin an academic career at the university where I met him. (He is still there—twenty years later.) He is an enthusiastic and effective teacher. When he saw no future at the university for classics, he retooled himself as a historian; when history became overcrowded, he switched to administration. I have tremendous respect for his talent and his adaptability.

As a husband, he was a calamity. He and his wife, Jennifer Anne, separated fifteen years ago. They have never divorced. Both Ted and Jenny were my friends when they were still together. And each of them spoke freely to me about the other. Jenny's story was that Ted simply tried too hard, that his love and his need to be loved overwhelmed her, that he was so committed to making the relationship ecstatically happy that neither of them could ever relax and enjoy the other. She put it simply: "Ted has this God-sized hole in his life, and he tried to fill it with me. I couldn't save him and neither could civil rights, the Kennedys, Pope John XXIII, the Peace Movement, the Human Potential Movement, or any of his other gods. I guess he should have stayed in the order. Even when they shunned him, he never lost his sense of the presence of God in his life. He says that he did, but that's not true. I knew him when he was in the order."

I knew him too. And I can document when he felt that he had lost hold of God or that God had lost hold of him. It happened long after he had been dispensed. He had been depressed about Jenny for more than a month. They had decided to separate. Then he thought that he was in love with one of his students. They became involved briefly, but he only felt more depressed. He told me that he just couldn't pray anymore—that God wasn't there for him.

Our friendship continued. Ted would talk about everything except Jenny or God. He and I were pals, confessors, brothers, and co-survivors. He visited me one summer when I was staying in an Atlantic shore community. We walked the beach, sharing academic war stories. What scars our laughter hid! But when I asked about Jenny, our laughter stopped.

He looked at the sea as he told me again of meeting and loving, of hoping and sharing, of parting and grieving, of life without comfort.

"But you still love Jenny," I said. "And she loves you. For God's sake, go back. Can you live without Jenny—without her love?"

He was lost in the sea, but he finally answered: "Jenny's love, what can I tell you of Jenny's love? I was a child when I met her, not even a child, I was the raw material of a man, dead substance waiting for the breath of God—dead substance—numb and useless. But Jenny loved *me*! And lavished on me such beauty, such tenderness, such faith that I became a man, the man that Jenny loved."

His fist smote the surf. "Lowell, there are demons in each of us. I don't mean 'evil spirits'; I mean that each of us is driven by forces within us that make us who we are. Take away what makes me distinct and I no longer exist. Stifle the obsessions that make Jenny who she is and you kill her. Once my demons tolerated her, and her demons tolerated mine. Now they bite and rend and tear us to bits.

"She knew," he continued, "Jenny always knew, and finally I realized that for Ted to be Ted and for Jenny to be Jenny our life together would have to end." He took a deep breath and said, "So it's over and done.

"I see her sometimes," he said, "see emptiness, feel pain—feel emptiness, see pain. But that's not all. I feel the warmth that was there once—that still is there for me—only for me. And something in me reaches out to find its home in her. But I call it back because I know to love Jen means destruction, to be loved by Jenny is to die—O God! How I miss the flames. Jenny, oh, Jenny, how I—"

And I held my friend, until his last tear, his very last tear for Jenny.

HEALING THE HEALER

At the inception of his public ministry, Jesus preached at the synagogue in his home town of Nazareth (Luke 4:16-30). From the several references made to healing in our Lord's sermon, we may safely infer that Jesus had already begun to perform the therapeutic miracles—the restoration of health and sanity—of which all four Evangelists speak. Anticipating the criticism that the out-of-town reports of the wonders he performed were exaggerated and knowing that his relatives' and neighbors' lack of faith would inhibit his power, Jesus declared, "Doubtless you will quote to me this proverb, 'Physician, heal yourself' " (Luke 4:23).

And I would echo these words to all who would counsel or advise others. Serving others as a counselor, adviser, or friend presupposes that the counselor is also being healed. I am not saying that the counselor *has been healed,* but that he or she *is being healed.* Salvation is recorded in the heavenly account books as a payment made once and for all, but in the here and now, it is an ongoing process. Paul, the staunchest advocate of the Good News that salvation is the gift of God that requires nothing of us but our acceptance, could demand that we work out our salvation with fear and trembling (Phil. 2:12).

The Christian life requires a constant openness on the part of the believer to the presence of God in his life, to the voice of God speaking to him as he responds to the needs of others. If you would help others, seek first to allow God to restore you moment by moment to wholeness and sanity. If you would be whole and sane, respond with the fullness of your being to the needs of others. But first the Christian counselor must be centered, focused, and grounded. Each of us has a spiritual "minimum daily requirement" of prayer, meditation, devotional reading, Bible study, and fellowship with other Christians. Before you or I can help others, we must be sure who we are, to whom we belong, to whom we are responsible, and what is the purpose of our lives.

Christian counselors see the big picture. They are responsive not only to the joys and sorrows of friends and neighbors, but are aware of the power available in each problem "both to will and to work for [God's] good pleasure" (Phil. 2:13). Christian counselors see the challenges and opportunities of life from a perspective that is set forth in the opening words of the Lord's Prayer: "Our Father in heaven— / May Your name be kept holy" (Matt. 6:9 Beck). These words imply the three essential rules by which Christian counselors live and serve others: (1) Let God be God, (2) accept responsibility, and (3) bind yourself to God in every act.

LET GOD BE GOD

We are all natural-born idolators. We displace what is ultimate with what demands our attention at a given moment in time. We act as though the gratification of our immediate needs is the most important thing in the world. The "me first" attitude—"I want mine and I want it now"—is the most prevalent form of idolatry.

Acting as though another human being or a group of human beings or a church or a book has all the answers is also idolatry. To depend totally on another person, doctrines, theological formulas, rituals, ethical norms may grant temporary comfort, but, in the end, easy answers cannot protect against tragedy, ambiguity, confusions, and injustice.

We are susceptible to idolatry especially during periods of scarcity, uncertainty, hopelessness, and boredom. When there is great want and frustration, men and women will turn to powers greater than themselves, to objects of love and adoration, to causes worth dying for. When established values break down and the future appears threatening, they will likewise turn away from all that they associate with suffering and anxiety and turn toward anyone or anything that seems to offer a way of escape.

Let God be God—I constantly must remind myself. Let nothing less than God receive my worship, my adoration, my dedication. Let all lesser gods—personal relationships, family, nation, vocation—bow before the true God. And let the true God be worshiped with all my being.

Let God be God. Let no orthodox doctrine or theological speculation or system of biblical interpretation or philosophical formulation about the divine be confused with God himself. And let no counselor forget that just as all descriptions of God fall short of their mark, so also all human solutions to human predicaments are limited. None of us comprehends all the variable and interacting factors, influences, and motivational forces that impact on an individual at a given moment. No form of intervention, no advice, no example is ever completely applicable, effectual, or decisive. To believe otherwise would be to grant ultimacy to the imperfect counsel of an imperfect being. The Christian counselor may be a wise and caring human, an exemplary human, a worthy human, but he or she is only human. Only God is God.

ACCEPT RESPONSIBILITY

We like to play victim. We want to blame someone or something for our failings and disappointments. I offer you my excuses and you accept them and offer yours in return. If you are temporarily out of excuses, you may borrow one or more from the following list.

I'm sorry that I failed to do what I promised but
—I was too busy,
—I had an unhappy childhood and you remind me
    of my father,
—I am allergic to yeast,
—I have low blood sugar,
—my parents were alcoholics and abused me when
    I was a child,
—I am going through an awkward stage,
—I am having an identity crisis,
—this is a really bad month for Capricorns,

—my spouse, children, and boss don't understand
   me,
—if God had wanted me to keep promises he would
   have put an alarm clock right in the middle of
   my forehead,
—what can you expect when the world is going to
   nuclear hell and the environment is being
   poisoned and we're only the pawns of the
   capitalistic system?
—and besides you should know that I really care
   and that not showing it is just the way I am.

A counselor has to make a fundamental decision
whenever he or she responds to another person: Am I
going to be *understanding* or am I going to be *effective*?
Am I going to *accept excuses* or am I going to *elicit change*?
If your purpose in life is to be liked, then you will want
to accept everyone's excuses. If you believe that you
have been called by God to make a difference in the lives
of those around you, you must be willing not to make or
to accept excuses. Jesus taught that our yes should mean
yes and our no mean no (Matt. 5:37; see also James
5:12).

I am not saying that there are not difficulties that
prevent us from keeping our word. A promise is an act
of faith—in oneself and in the future. And sometimes
this faith proves unjustified. We all miss the mark now
and then. We try and we fail. Or our good intentions are
thwarted by unforeseen circumstances. No one can
govern the future, but all of us can decide what our yes
and no means. And we can decide what we will expect of
others. When you give your word do you intend to keep
it? Or do you give it because your friends want you to
and you want them to like you? When your friends give
their word to you, do you convey to them your
expectation that they will do what they say? Or do they
already know that you expect them to fail, that you will

understand, and that their excuses will always be accepted?

BIND YOURSELF TO GOD IN EVERY ACT

At the Last Supper, Jesus spoke of "the new covenant in my blood which is shed for many for the remission of sins." No doubt, Jesus had in mind the words of the prophet Jeremiah:

Behold, the days are coming, says the Lord, when I will make a new covenant with the house of Israel and the house of Judah, not like the covenant which I made with their fathers when I took them by the hand to bring them out of the land of Egypt. . . . But this is the covenant which I will make with the house of Israel after those days, says the Lord: I will put my law within them, and I will write it upon their hearts; and I will be their God, and they shall be my people. And no longer shall each man teach his neighbor and each his brother, saying, "Know the Lord," for they shall all know me, from the least of them to the greatest, says the Lord; for I will forgive their iniquity, and I will remember their sin no more (Jer. 31:31-34).

The covenant of Sinai was a contract between God and his chosen people. It was restricted to one nation, to a few hundred thousand souls. God promised to bind himself to this people, and they reciprocated by becoming a separate nation, a holy priesthood, a peculiar people—special because every act of their lives would be a sacrament, a holy ritual, a sign of their unique relationship to God.

But at the Last Supper, Jesus spoke of "the new covenant in my blood which is shed for many for the remission of sins." The new covenant is open to all. It is written in our hearts and is manifested in the tenderness of our consciences and our dedication to love and serve our brothers and sisters.

However, to say that the new covenant is written in our hearts does not mean that it is simply a matter of emotions or feelings. Being children of the new covenant does not excuse us from the call of God to bind ourselves to him in every act and deed so that in our lives as individuals, as families, and as communities of faith, we shall be known for our separateness, our commitment, our honesty, our integrity, and our love for others. The new covenant does not replace the old. It fulfills it in lives that reflect the presence of the God-given second nature.

In the old covenant there was no gap between sacred and profane, between holy and secular. There was a divinely prescribed way to eat, sleep, dress, work, and worship. Every act had the potential of sanctifying the individual, binding him or her to God and revealing his or her covenant with God. For the child of the new covenant, there is likewise no separation between secular and profane activities. God is with us and in us, luring us to be his partners, using us as prisms through which the light of his presence may be seen by others. As imperfect as we may be, something in us has died with the Christ to the self-centered life so that the Christ-nature may flourish in each of us in every thought, word, and deed.

To hallow the name of God is to live in such a way that what one believes is obvious. The most effective witness is borne not by those who recite biblical passages and utter "praise the Lord" and "glory to Jesus" at every opportunity but by those who put their faith into action. The presence of God in the world is the glue that holds all things together; the dimension of depth that enhances every truly human experience; the sense of mystery, wonder, and awe that spontaneously surprises us again and again. The divine presence is a gift that we do not deserve and yet our own attainment and accomplishment. I know that the central question in my own life is how much depends on circumstances and how much on my own efforts. Again and again, it has been my experience that I have achieved what would not have been attained if I had not singlemindedly sought to achieve it and yet I am aware that the effort had little to do with the result. I work as though everything depends on my work, but I discover again and again that I am the recipient of unmerited favor. For God is present when we make the decision that our lives will have purpose and meaning, when we bestow purpose and meaning on the lives of others. And, regardless of what we do or attempt, God's presence is a highly contagious infection that we catch from and give to others. Those chosen as "carriers" are Christian counselors.

CHAPTER 2

Getting Down to Basics

WHAT IS COUNSELING?

For a moment, let's consider some of the basic terms we have been using up to this point: counseling and Christian. In its narrower sense, counseling refers to the interaction between individuals and specialized professionals such as mental health practitioners and lawyers. If my friend Mark says to me, "This morning I saw a counselor," I would assume that he meant a psychiatrist, psychologist, or social worker. If Walter and I were having lunch, and Walter waved to someone a few feet away and said "Hello, counselor," I would assume the third party was an attorney. Obviously, this book is neither a guide to psychology nor to the law. Mental health professionals serve many deep needs, but, for the most part, the real job of counseling is done on a day-to-day basis by the supportive friend, relative, and other caring individual who may not know Sigmund Freud from Fred Flintstone but who puts himself or herself on the line as one human being responding to another.

A counselor, as the term is used in this book, is simply one who gives advice to others. To counsel is to enter into a caring relationship with another, and, on the basis of that relationship, to recommend, suggest, urge, advise, caution, evaluate, recommend, and reprove. To counsel is also to elicit change, to become an agent of transformation in the lives of others.

Counseling another person can be done either explicitly or implicitly. Advice can be explicit; that is, it can take the form of spoken or written recommendations. For example, if my friend asks me what to do about her teenage son's lack of interest in high school, I can suggest various remedies—tell her to hire a tutor, urge her to help her son with his homework, point out that the young man watches too much television. I can invite her son to my house and try to find out why he is ignoring his studies. Perhaps I would discover that he is enthusiastic about other possible courses of study and that a change of courses should be encouraged. Or perhaps I will learn that conflicts with his parents or romantic problems or peer pressures (or all of the above) are the real culprits and that talking them out with a supportive, nonjudgmental adult (other than his parents) is just the ticket for him. Or I could write a letter to my young friend's homeroom teacher offering my suggestions.

Most counseling is neither direct nor obvious. Sometimes it is not even intentional. When I was ten, a friend of my parents, who was aware of my interest in religious stories, gave me a copy of *Bulfinch's Mythology*. Two years later, the same friend provided me with a collegiate dictionary. He made no direct recommendations about what I should study or what career orientation I should adopt. He didn't advise me to earn a Ph.D. in religion or to become a writer. Such thoughts never entered his mind. Yet the implicit encouragment of these two books had a great deal to do with the path that I eventually followed. He was a more effective counselor than he realized!

When I was eighteen, I worked as an editor at a well-known Bible college. I spent a great deal of time with Charles, a professor of Old Testament studies, who was continually recommending books for me to read, inviting me to accompany him to meetings of scholarly societies, introducing me to his professional colleagues in the most flattering manner, offering to teach me foreign languages, and writing letters of recommendation so that I might obtain a scholarship to attend a major university. By sharing his own personal history with me, he helped me understand that the words "Christian" and "scholar" were not contradictory. His advice was direct and supportive. At a critical point in my life, he enabled me to feel that I had a future. He helped me gain momentum to pursue my potential, to risk changing my life, when it would have been much more convenient for me to stay in my comfortable and unchallenging rut.

I also remember Elizabeth, my supervisor in the editorial department, a woman fifty years my senior. She scolded me when my attention drifted from my duties, demanded virtual perfection of me in copy editing and proofreading, while defending me to her superior when three typographical errors surfaced in one of my projects, "One error every hundred pages is quite acceptable," she contended. She was the embodiment of the Protestant work ethic, an example of personal integrity and dedication. She freely shared with me how she had developed into the person that she was, how her faith and her understanding had matured. I remember in particular her anecdotes about opportunities she had spurned (in order to care for an invalid mother who lived to age ninety-five) and the price she had paid. She recommended to her superiors that I succeed her when she retired and, at the same time, offered to lend me the money for college tuition if

I would quit my job and return to school. Her explicit
suggestions were few and far between. She never
praised me to my face or in the presence of others. Yet
to this day, I still encounter mutual acquaintances from
those days thirty years ago, who tell me of the kind and
complimentary remarks about me that she was accustomed to make.

Charles and Elizabeth were Christians. But so were
the other thousand employees at the firm. After all, it
was a Bible institute. Charles and Elizabeth were
counselors—not because of any special training or
certification but because inspiring and motivating
young adults came naturally to them. Through word,
deed, and example, they encouraged me to envision
what could be and to attempt it. There was a special
relatedness, a bond, between Charles and Elizabeth and
myself. And although they have been dead for many
years, their encouragement continues as an active force
in my life.

WHO IS A CHRISTIAN?

Who is a Christian? And how is a Christian counselor
different from a Jewish counselor? Or a Hindu
counselor? Or a Zen Buddhist counselor? Or the
agnostic counselor? Or the atheistic counselor? This
book is addressed to those who identify themselves with
the gospel of Jesus Christ, however they may understand such identification. I am presupposing in these
pages a certain perspective or point of view as a basis for
counseling others. It is possible to offer sound advice to
others, be a compassionate and caring person, significantly influence others for the better without having
any religious or spiritual convictions. And it is just as
possible to have numerous degrees from theological

institutions, belong to every church in town, attend seminars on spirituality, memorize the Bible from cover to cover, and still be conspicuously lacking in both compassion for others and the tactfulness required to influence their lives.

Who is a Christian? It is best to leave the ultimate answer with God. As Jesus insisted, "Not everyone who calls Me Lord, Lord, will get into the kingdom of heaven, only he who does what My Father in heaven wants" (Matt. 7:21 Beck). For me, a Christian is one who believes that God was active in the world in the person of Jesus of Nazareth, that the person and work of Jesus are unique, and that Jesus reconciles us to God and to one another. I cannot state much about the historic Jesus and yet I know that I strive after the realization of my own Christ-nature and that I feel Jesus of Nazareth is my partner in the striving. I believe that God is present in the world, luring us to partnership, revealing in community ever higher and deeper levels of what it means to be truly human.

I believe that God is available, that he possesses us and lures us toward himself. And I believe that he acts in, through, and despite the church—in, through, and despite me as well.

THE COUNSELOR'S ATTITUDE

Case Notes: *Wilmer*

A few years ago, I was speaking to an adult education group at a church not too far from my home. Wilmer, a member of the audience, frequently interrupted, pontificating about the subject on which I was speaking, a subject in which he was not particularly well versed. He soon became aware of how annoying he was and began defending himself at such length and with such intensity that my original irritation with his interruptions was exacerbated. When I

tried to continue with my presentation, he started making
statements such as, "Well, of course, I don't have a theological
degree or a Ph.D., but I'm a graduate of the school of hard
knocks." Finally, without anyone challenging his increasingly
defensive assertions, he stormed out of the building. After
the session, I was talking with the pastor about his
parishioner's display of bad manners and my uncomfortable
feeling about it. He explained to me that the man was "retired
military" who was raised by an "overbearing and unaffec-
tionate father," that he had "a type A personality," and that if
I had known this I would have "understood" that the man's
rudeness was "just the way he is." The pastor added that the
man had been acting this way for years and that no one in the
congregation paid any attention to him. What a shame. For
the congregation's "understanding" of Wilmer guarantees
that he will be both rude and lonely for the rest of his life.

The Wilmers of this world always make me ask myself
what attitude should govern counseling. Should we learn
everything that we can about human behavior and
interpersonal relationships? Or should we just be
ourselves and respond immediately and intuitively to the
needs of others? The answer to both questions is yes.
What is required is a balance of objective perspective and
personal involvement. The more we know about what
makes people tick, how society works, what the Bible
teaches, the more adequately we can respond. (And the
more fully we respond, the more fully we come to know.)
But if our knowledge of others is a collection of static
"one size fits all" generalizations, a limited number of
concepts and categories into which we try to stuff
everyone so that we do not have to deal with who they are
and what they require of us, our data is useless. Love
without understanding is dangerous and knowledge
without commitment is like having a pantry full of
canned food but no can opener. Something wonderful
may be in there, but it is of no use to anyone.

According to Martin Buber's familiar distinction, human beings are capable of two basic attitudes toward reality, *I-It* and *I-You*.[1] When we regard the realities that we daily experience as objects to be understood, utilized, dominated, or controlled, the *I-It* attitude is paramount. There is nothing wrong with this attitude. Without the perspective of *I-It*, we would be unable to respond to the world in which we find ourselves. To perceive, to feel, to imagine, to will, to think—all of these *I-It* relations are essential operations of our routine existence.

The attitude of *I-You* designates a relationship between subjects or persons. Although I live by virtue of my *I-It* objectivity, it is only when I respond to another being as "you" and am myself so responded to that my distinctive nature, my life as a person in relation to another person, is realized.

That which happens between and an *I* and a *You* determines the uniqueness of each person, the never-to-be-repeated meaning of his or her life. It is through the *I-You* relationship that personality emerges. For the *I* that exists apart from the web of interpersonal relations scarcely has substance at all. It is through *I-You* relationships that my distinctive selfhood is born and lives. The more fully and genuinely I relate to the *you* whom I meet, the more determinately real I become, the more communication is transformed into communion, existing into living.

I-You experience is marked by immediacy, spontaneity, directness, and intensity. Regardless of what has occurred in the past, when I confront you without the protective armor of my preconceptions and prejudices,

---

1. Martin Buber, *I and Thou* (New York: Charles Scribner's Sons, 1958) and *Between Man and Man* (New York: Macmillan, 1965). See also the present writer, *The Promise of Buber* (Philadelphia: J. B. Lippincott Co., 1969).

the astonishing and inconceivable flashes between us are like static electricity.

Where life touches life deeply, each person achieves an extent of personal development that otherwise remains hidden and unrealized. As I respond to your unique nature, I discover for myself and reveal to you who I really am, and you discover for yourself and reveal to me who you really are. Only through such relationships can the healing, teaching, reforming, and redeeming of persons as individuals or as members of society be accomplished.

No moment of our life is purely *I-You* or *I-It.* The two attitudes are inextricably interwoven. There is the *you* that I know as a sum of qualities, a certain physical shape with certain features, observed patterns of behavior, habitual ways of reacting to given situations. Such knowledge or understanding of you as an object or *it,* gives me a secure, predictable basis on which to build a relationship. For if you changed drastically from moment to moment, there would be no real *you* for me to relate to. But my image of you is imperfect—a picture that constantly reacts with the unique, unpredictable *you* of our relationship. No matter how thoroughly I know you and myself, I can never fully know what will happen *between* us.

In the meeting of person with person, there are possibilities for mutual growth and personal satisfaction that other experiences lack. As two persons come to know each other intimately, to react to each other, and to find their true selves reflected in the other, something more than the addition of person and person is happening. Something intrigues and attracts them. There is a third partner in all *I-You* relationships. In my response to the you of my life, I am drawn to ever higher levels of mutual self-realization and satisfaction. *This lure is the Eternal Thou.* Out of the multiplicity of

I-You meetings, there emerges not only the picture of who I am and who the other is, but of the ally who addresses us and calls us to partnership.

Life is hallowed and bound to God whenever persons brood over their personal and interpersonal lives, seeking to open them to the creative presence of the divine. All things wait to be hallowed, to be brought into living mutual relationship.

A sympathetic person who asks another, "Where does it hurt?" and, "What can I do to help?" accomplishes more than the most highly knowledgeable student of psychology, sociology, theology, or any other "–ology." Counseling is a demanding job. One minute it requires all the learning, zeal, understanding, kindness that you can muster; the next minute it reveals that you have much to learn and that your own ego and personal needs interfere with your best efforts.

One minute it requires that we "understand" our friends, that we have a satisfactory store of categories with which to interpret their behavior. The next minute it demands that we forget everything we thought we knew so that we may listen and respond with an intensity we never knew we had.

And when both knowledge and personal involvement fail, the Christian counselor turns, humbly and expectantly, to the third partner in every dialogue, the Eternal Thou.

CHAPTER 3

The Counselor's Gospel

THE KINGDOM IS HERE AND NOW AND YET TO COME

The Four Gospels proclaim the Good News that God is with us, that his kingdom is *here* and *now* and *yet to come*. The kingdom is *here,* the Four Evangelists announce, in the person and work of Jesus of Nazareth. Through his chosen one, we learn, God is invading our existence, transforming (and complicating) our lives, taking us as partners, surrendering himself to our state and fate, giving us the opportunity to transcend suffering, tragedy, and death. God is calling and choosing us as recruits to his kingdom, deepening our capacity to feel all human emotions, forcing us to contend with enhanced ups and cruel downs. God gives us life more abundant, ecstatic, and fruitful even as we come to know the enemies of life—pain, disappointment, and failure—more intensely than ever.

The kingdom of God is *here,* the Gospels declare, because the King is here. The kingdom is *now* because the presence of God in our lives as Christians is unavoidable. God has broken into our daily existence, changed our nature, and empowered us. We are neither better nor worse than other human beings. In a sense, our lives are more difficult, more complex.

Whether we want it or not, there is a sensitivity, a responsiveness to the divine in our lives. In the Synoptic Gospels (Matthew, Mark, and Luke), God's new rule begins with the healing by Jesus of the emotionally disturbed (Matt. 4:23-25; Mark 1:21-27; Luke 5:31). The divine plan requires that the chosen one both reveal and conceal himself. The disguised King allows his subjects to guess at his identity and at what lies in store for them during his future reign. Jesus hides his vision of a new age in parables while he divulges it by healing the sick, restoring discards to their rightful place in humanity's embrace, and annulling death's claims.

Who Jesus really is bursts through, at the outset of his public career, in what he does for those whose bizarre and undisciplined behavior has made them the outcasts, rejects, and pariahs of their time. The writers of the first three Gospels called them demon-possessed or spirit-afflicted. We today might describe them as crazy, schizophrenic, manic depressive, addicts, or derelicts. The labels by which such individuals are known are not important. What matters is that in every age and in every place—at the time of Jesus and in our own time—such individuals are unloved and unwanted in the society of "normal" human beings. And no matter how much their actions contribute to the reactions they receive, the fact remains that they experience that lack of love as bitterly as any rejection can be felt.

Whether one is a psychopath or a saint, not being loved hurts. We should know. None of us were that lovable when God called us. "We love," John tells us in his First Letter, "because he first loved us" (I John 4:19). The kingdom of God is *now* whenever and wherever there is love, caring, and compassion for those previously spurned, ignored, and neglected. And that includes us and those to whom we respond.

It is interesting to note that the Fourth Gospel does not emphasize the healing of demoniacs at all. John chooses to recount only seven miracles or signs. The first is the changing of water into wine at the wedding in Cana of Galilee (John 2). The others are the healing of a man who had been ill of an unspecified illness for thirty-eight years (John 5:2-9), the feeding of the five thousand (6:10-14), giving sight to a blind man (9:1-12), raising Lazarus from the dead (11:38-44), and, finally, the resurrection of Jesus (John 20). John is preoccupied with symbolism. The wondrous wine of Cana is clearly a reference to the wine of the Eucharist even as the multiplied loaves speak of the bread of the Lord's Supper. The illness, blindness, and death that Jesus conquers are really the sin of all humankind and its consequences. The marriage at Cana is representative of all Christian marriage; it is sanctified only when Jesus is present. John shows little concern for the individuals who received the benefits of the miracles. He does not offer us the rich vignettes, full of expressive dialogue and weighty characterizations by which the interaction between Jesus and those who sought his help are described in the other Gospel accounts. Not once does John tell us that Jesus insisted on faith as a basis for what he did. For John's focus is on the One who performs the wonders and what they signify.

For John, the kingdom is not of this world; yet he affirms that the struggles with sickness and death, the happiness of each wedding day, even the hunger for our daily bread point us to a spiritual reality that underlies, impregnates, and transcends our ordinary existence. The person "who has the Son has life" and has it in abundance. And the fullness of that life pours out in acts of loving service. Jesus washes the feet of his followers, weeps at the death of a beloved friend, finds a home for his mother even as he dies on the cross, comforts the grieving Mary Magdalene merely by speaking her name on Easter morning, and cooks breakfast for the disciples after the resurrection. The sermons and parables of Jesus found in Matthew, Mark, and Luke make clear what is expected of us as citizens of the kingdom. Somehow John best tells us why.

The kingdom of God is *coming*. It is always beyond our grasp. It lures us like some beautiful butterfly that we would snare for our collection, and then it eludes us. As God's partners, we are able to actualize it for brief moments here and there. We are used as instruments of peace. We find love that we do not deserve or understand. We serve others and are served by others. We are lured on and on by a love that will not let us go. But the age in which we live dooms us to frustration, suffering, loneliness, and death. So why bother? Why care? Why love? Surely we will be misunderstood, humiliated, and rejected—no matter how pure our motives may be. Our own failings and limitations will ultimately negate everything we accomplish. This world's cacophony of greed, lust, and selfishness will drown out our quiet songs of faith, hope, and charity. And, finally, each of us will die and be forgotten. The unfeeling world machine will grind on remorselessly— war after war, death after death, calamity after calamity.

Until the new age. Until the promise made by God in the Messiah's death and resurrection is kept. Someday, the Christian faith boldly affirms, we will study war no more. Someday peace will prevail not only in the affairs of nations but the petty differences that set people against one another. There will be no more angry words, no feeling that what you have should be mine, no shortage of caring, no lack of love, no divorce, no selfishness, no theft, no victims. Someday nature will not be at odds with humankind or humankind with nature. Someday there will be no disease, no famine, no earthquakes, no tidal waves, no hurricanes. And, finally, individuals will no longer be at war with themselves. Loneliness, frustration, fear, stress, meaninglessness, and confusion will be forgotten like so many discarded fashions.

How do we know that all this will be so? That we will beat our swords into plowshares? That what we lost in the fall of Adam will be restored through the Christ, the founder of a new race? That God will be all in all? We don't *know*. We, as Christians, have taken the Jesus of the Gospels at his word. From the world's point of view, we are fools, simpletons, and children. We wait for God's inevitable triumph, tasting it, longing for it, spying it through the murk of everyday struggle, and affirming it in our prayers: ". . . your kingdom come, your will be done."

And now and then, that kingdom is real and present for us. As we mentioned above, Jesus began his ministry by restoring the spurned to human fellowship. When out of gratitude, those whom he returned to sanity tried to join his traveling company, he ordered them to remain in the home towns to which they rightfully belonged. Jesus healed hundreds, perhaps thousands. But those whom he called to give up their families, friends, and vocations for the sake of "full-time Christian service" were limited to a handful. It is easy to use the excuse of being a Christian to avoid the really hard job of being a human being, belonging to a family, living in a community, but the kingdom that Jesus proclaims requires very few of us to do anything else. Of course, how we are human, how we are part of our families, how we respond to the needs of our neighbors makes all the difference in the world.

PART II

THE COUNSELOR'S VOCATION

*Our daily bread—give it to us today;
And forgive us our debts as we indeed have
already forgiven our debtors (Matt. 6:12
LDS).*

*And forgive us our sins, as we indeed
forgive everyone indebted to us; and do not
lead us into temptation (Luke 11:4 LDS).*

You heard that it was said to the ancients:
"You shall not kill; and whoever kills, shall be
liable to judgment." But I tell you that
everyone who is angry with his brother shall
be liable to judgment, and whoever calls his
brother a "stupid idiot," shall be liable to stand
before the Sanhedrin [the council of tribal
elders]; and whoever calls his brother a
"dumb moron," shall be liable to the burning
garbage heap. Therefore, if you bring your
gift to the altar and there remember that your
brother has something against you, leave your
gift there at the altar, and go first and be
reconciled to your brother, and then come

and offer your gift (Matt. 5:21-24 LDS).
Now if your brother sins, go reprove him between you and him alone. If he listens to you, you have gained your brother. But if he does not listen, take with you one or two more, that by the mouth of two or three witnesses every matter may be established; but if he refuses to listen to them, tell it to the church; and if he refuses to listen even to the church, let him be to you as a Gentile and a tax collector (Matt. 18:15-17 LDS).

Dress up, therefore, as chosen ones of God, holy and beloved, with hearts of compassion, kindness, humility, gentleness, patience, forbearing one another and forgiving one another. If anyone has a complaint against another, as indeed the Lord forgave you so also should you (Col. 3:12-13 LDS).

CHAPTER 4

The Counselor's Vocation

Case Notes: *Maggie*

Alan, who is our friend and our insurance agent, was our dinner guest a few months ago. We were discussing "hard-to-love" people. Alan told us about Maggie, a one-time friend of his. He described her as follows:

Maggie is an elementary schoolteacher, who was a friend of mine for ten years. She is attractive, vivacious, and articulate. She is also a pain in the neck. She constantly makes promises but never keeps them.

When my family moved into a new house, she promised that she would buy an expensive house-warming gift, would bake a casserole dinner, would have a friend of hers help plan a Japanese garden. She did not do any of these things.

When my son was in the hospital recuperating from surgery, she said that she would visit him daily, would play chess with him, and would ask her father, a prominent orthopedic surgeon, to look in on the boy. None of this transpired.

When my wife died of cancer, Maggie said that she would handle all the arrangements and that she would see to it that she spent time with me to help me sort out my feelings. I thanked her for the gesture but acted as though it had never been made. As usual, she did nothing.

Wilma

Wilma was an executive secretary at a firm with which I did business. She was a chronic latecomer. On Monday, she was twenty minutes late. She said that she had been delayed by an emergency phone call from her mother in Houston. Her boss accepted her excuse and told her to be sure not to be late again. On Tuesday, she was twenty minutes late and had new excuses. Her daughter had misplaced her homework and Wilma had helped her find it. The boss was understanding and told her that it was essential that she be on time the next day since he was expecting a visit from his boss. On Wednesday, she was thirty minutes late and blamed it on a multi-vehicle accident on the freeway.

Finally, her long-suffering boss suggested that she start a half an hour later and reduce her lunch break from sixty to thirty minutes. She agreed and promised to be on time. When they tried the new schedule, she was still an average of twenty minutes late per day. One of her children would suddenly get sick or her husband would need his shirt reironed or there would be an overnight power failure in her neighborhood or her car would break down.

TV OR NOT TV?

I purchased a portable television from a local store, which was part of a major discount chain. It worked fine in the store but when I got it home, the picture rolled incessantly and no amount of adjustment could stop it. Since the set was under warranty, I returned it to the store. It was repaired and returned to me. The picture still rolled. After four attempts to have the TV repaired, I asked the salesperson for a refund or a credit. He explained that both were out of the question. The set was now used and out of warranty and besides the problem was in the manufacturer's design. His company was well aware that the set had "inadequate horizontal circuitry" but, he added, "there is nothing that we can do about it." I suggested that his firm could stop selling television sets that did not work, threw the offending set in the garbage, and bought a new set from a different merchant.

Within a few days, a serious distortion developed in the bottom half of the image. The performer who appeared on the screen looked as though their legs were three times as long as their upper torsos. The salesperson explained that the set had "inadequate vertical circuitry," made some comments abut "cheap junk from the Orient," and asked, "What do you expect for eighty bucks?" Fourteen years later, the set sits forlornly alone, unused, and unwanted in my garage.

I decided to subscribe to a consumer protection magazine so that in the future I could tell good products from bad products. I sent a check, which was processed, but I never got my magazine. For four years, I wrote, phoned, begged, pleaded, cajoled, sent photocopies of the canceled check—all to no avail.

The counselor's vocation is dealing with failure, sin, and broken promises. Counselors do this by offering advice, fostering personal transformation, and encouraging independence. Their faith, understanding of the human condition, and skills as peacemakers and advisers are their "daily bread."

Christian counselors are in the sin and forgiveness business. They receive forgiveness wholesale and distribute it retail. And both the supply and the demand are inexhaustible. The first time a Christian counsels another person, he or she becomes aware of the depth and persistence of human perversity. That perversity should seem familiar to Christians—it is so much like their own. For each of us seems to want diametric opposites all the time. We will not allow ourselves to be content. Our ability to grasp defeat from the jaws of victory, to turn happiness into misery, to act contrary to our own self-interests is astonishing.

It is simple to explain drug addiction, shyness, depression, anxiety, sexual promiscuity, lack of assertion, suicidal behavior, or cult involvement as manifestations of low self-esteem, but that presupposes that there is a readily available alternative. The problem is that most "normal, well-adjusted" people do not seem to like themselves any more than those known to be at risk. Not only is there an epidemic of inferiority complexes but the fact is most of these complexes are totally justified. For when it comes to any standard that we would set for ourselves, we fall short.

It takes more than faith in God and commitment to his kingdom to make one either a Christian or a counselor. It requires awareness of human perversity, the sinfulness not only of those whom we counsel but of ourselves as counselors. Sin is breaking the rules. Sin is missing the mark. Sin is failure to keep one's word. Sin is refusal to accept responsibility for one's words and acts. Sin is living as though other persons are supposed to honor their commitments but excusing ourselves for not keeping ours.

God made a contract with Adam and Eve. They broke it. God made a covenant with the nation Israel. They turned to other gods and neglected the demands of justice to which they had pledged themselves. Jesus the Christ offered the new covenant sealed with his blood, a community of Spirit-endowed brothers and sisters whose life would manifest the lordship of God. We as Christians have committed ourselves to live by our Lord's example of self-sacrifice and service. We have given our word by voluntarily accepting membership in the church and by repeatedly participating in its worship and sacraments. But do we keep our word?

Sin is deluding ourselves into believing that it is all right not to honor our commitments. Sin is each of us accepting his or her own feeble excuses—everybody else does it, it really doesn't make any difference, I'm only one person, I'm only human, rules are made to be broken, there are always exceptions, the other person will understand that I was too busy.

Sin is refusing to honor one's word. To put it a somewhat different way, sin is dodging responsibility. "Why did you disobey my instructions?" God asked Adam in the Garden of Eden. Adam's response, a classic of shifting the blame, was, "The woman you gave me—she told me to."

I learned a long time ago that I would never know for sure whether what I believed was true or false, so I would have to decide for myself how I was going to live. Was I going to live as though there were a just and loving God? As though I were accountable for my actions? As though I could make a difference in my own life and in the lives of others? Or was I going to live a life of excuses?

I wonder if any society at any time in history has entertained more excuses, more ways to dodge responsibility. Look at the role of psychiatric witnesses in criminal trials. Without going into details about some of the more celebrated cases such as those of the Hillside Strangler, Dan White, and Patty Hearst, let me point out that the acceptance of the notion that individuals are machines that are programmed by circumstances and triggered by stress into committing horrendous acts for which these machines are not responsible is the inevitable culmination of the accepting of excuses.

As a counselor, I long ago abandoned as my goal the "understanding" of my client, that is, the assigning of external causes that enabled them to blame their present distress on someone or something else. Everything that counselors know about a friend helps them do their job. But, primarily, the counselor is in the business of facilitating change in the lives of those who want to change and of motivating the desire for change in the lives of those who are not yet ready.

Jesus had a special contempt for those he called hypocrites—those who professed a standard of conduct, condemned others who fell short of the mark, but excused themselves from the wholehearted observance of the rules of the game. He made clear that attending religious services, giving money to charity, even preaching and working miracles in his name could not substitute for doing what the Father wants. And what does God want? The words are simple: justice, mercy, humility, love, service. Every moment of every day is a demand, an invitation, an opportunity. We may respond with the wholeness of our being, accept responsibility, commit ourselves or we can drift from one immediate satisfaction to the next, forever justifying the unjustifiable, excusing the inexcusable.

The wages of sin is death. Paul tells us that in the sixth chapter of Romans. Death is being cut off from the love of others as the result of our selfishness. Death is ending up with no character at all because the excuses that we offer become more real to our family and friends than the deeds that express who we are. Death is a society without direction in which everyone is for himself or herself. Death is life without a sense that what I do counts, that I stand for something, that my acts, deeds, and work are of value. Death is always having to be right and ending up right and alone forever.

The gift of God is life—abundant life, life of the ages, life energized by the presence of God himself, life shared and replenished in a community of brothers and sisters. The faith that saves us from death is not a momentary rush of excitement, although it certainly may start or be nurtured there. Faith is faithfulness, commitment, realizing that life is precious and significant. Faith is living as though it is natural that I will keep my word, that I will do the job for which I am being paid, that I will stop running off at the mouth with self-pitying lamentations, and that I will open my ears and my heart to those to whom I have pledged myself, including my brothers and sisters in Christ.

The payoff for keeping one's word, for accepting responsibility, for responding with love and concern? The payoff for living as though there is a just and loving God is that we *experience* a just and loving God. By living as though our individual lives have significance and meaning, they *have* significance and meaning. By acting and speaking as though the church to which we belong is a community of those who bear one another's burdens, that church *becomes* a community of those who bear one another's burdens.

CHAPTER 5

The Counselor as Adviser

Case Notes: *Mary Lou*

Mary Lou could have been the poster girl for depression. Every day in class, she sat slumped, dejected, and morose. Getting her to participate in discussion was so exhausting for me as the teacher that I quickly gave up.

After class one day, I told her how frustrating it was for me to try to guess who she was and what was on her mind. I asked her if she could write a one-page essay, telling me, "Four things I know about myself."

The next day, she arrived with an armload of typing paper to which she had glued photographs of models from a dozen different mass-circulation women's magazines. She placed them on the floor in a meandering pattern like the tracks of a toy train. I stooped over and walked from photo to photo. The young women in the ads were thin, happy, and conventionally attractive. Mary Lou was dumpy and plain. She would never look like the models in those magazines.

Carol

Carol had become a rebellious child—at age twenty-two. She suddenly dropped out of the university, moved in with a sleazy drug dealer, and began selling her body in bars. "She's never done anything like this before," her heartbroken mother told me. "Why, she was always a perfect child—a debutante and a member of my old sorority." I had been visiting the family when they learned of Carol's behavior. While we were talking one evening, the family insisted that I see Carol's room. It was supposed to tell me how much they loved her and what good parents they had been. The room was furnished like an expensive dollhouse—all ruffles, lace, antiques, and delicate bric-a-brac. I could not imagine a human being living there.

Probably because she had known me for years, Carol agreed to let me try to help reconcile her with her parents. After several sessions, I told her that she seemed as determined at age twenty-two to not do what her parents wanted her to do as she had been during her childhood and adolescent years to do what they wanted her to do. She suddenly realized that her life was just as controlled by her parents when she rebelled against them as it was when she had been their dutiful, perfect child. She stopped taking drugs, broke up with her boyfriend, and moved to another city.

Her mother thanked me for what had been accomplished, but her father became angry with me for not having convinced her to return home so that she could live in her old room and attend a local college. Five years later, when Carol, who still had not earned a college degree, married a struggling gold prospector, her dad let me know (through a mutual friend) that he disapproved of the match, and that, once again, he held me responsible.

Marilyn

Marilyn was a beautiful, outgoing woman who made friends easily with men and women. Her friends cared deeply for her and remained devoted for many years. But Marilyn had one serious flaw. She turned her relationships with the men in her life into operatic tragedies. Each of her four husbands ended up beating her savagely and, finally, leaving her. I knew all four of the men and none of them appeared to fit the wife-beating role. They told me (and Marilyn confirmed) that she was obsessed with the notion that all men would eventually turn on her and desert her. In a letter that she sent me, she blamed her expectations on her own parents' marriage. Her father had been an alcoholic who had badly abused his long-suffering wife. Marilyn claimed that this was the only picture she had of what a man was like. Whether the tragedies of her life were caused by her own behavior, the weaknesses of the men she married, or both, there seemed to be a controlling fantasy behind the whole drama—Marilyn's prophecy that all men would be like her father.

After her fourth divorce, Marilyn was hospitalized for acute alcoholism. Ironically, she was treated in the same ward as her father who had died there twenty years earlier.

GIVING ADVICE AND ELICITING CHANGE

When Moses asked the name of God, the voice from the burning bush responded: "I AM WHO I AM." In God, promise and fulfillment are one. God keeps his word. He is his word.

Counseling is the restoration of men and women to their true freedom as children of God, as those in whom promise and fulfillment are also one. Counselors do not passively wait for their advice to be sought, nor do they intrude in the lives of strangers with the truth whether they want it or not.

THE MEANING OF FREEDOM

Mary Lou had accepted the suggestion that only the thin and beautiful are worthy of love. Carol confused freedom with doing what her parents didn't want her to do. Marilyn destroyed her own life so that she could prove that her father was a bastard. Each of them was in a trance. None was fully conscious or alive. None of them was free.

Our conception of freedom is simple and basic. Freedom is the power to decide and to accept responsibility for one's decisions. The human will is never free of influences. We are all coerced to a significant degree by our memories, upbringing, education, by the responses and expectations of those with whom we interact, and by the society in which we live. Free individuals are those who amidst all the circumstances that condition and limit their freedom, see the difference between necessary and unnecessary influences and choose which they will follow.

Freedom is responsible decision making—acting and accepting the consequences for one's actions. To be free, one must learn to overcome undue and unfair influences of manipulative groups and persuasive individuals as well as the "hidden persuaders"—the appeals of advertisers, the half-truths of politicians, the oversimplifications of the mass media, and the prejudices that we harbor against all that is alien to us. Moreover, one must be careful not to exchange one form of dependency for another.

Counseling is the process by which unexamined assumptions are challenged and a shift in perception is stimulated that enables our friends to tell the truth about themselves and awaken from their trance states. What trance states? Most of the time we are unconscious of the fact that we long to be dependent, are desperately striving to be dependent, are living only for the coming of that strong figure who will comfort, protect, and guide us while freeing us from the responsibility for our own acts. Thus, we are susceptible daily to being controlled by individuals, social institutions, the government, the media, advertising. For we are really responding automatically to the internalized parental figures whose love, acceptance, praise, and approval we crave.

Christians who act as counselors attempt to wake their friends from the trance of their everyday lives. They guide their friends into reexamining their assumptions and setting aside myths, exaggerations, and hysteria. For example, parents with a "problem" child must be urged to reevaluate their presuppositions about their child and about themselves as parents. Who is really the problem? They must be trained to listen to their child, to abandon approaches such as guilt-tripping ("Do you know what you're doing to your mother and me? How can you do this to us?") and insults ("How can you be so stupid? What's wrong with you?"), which widen the gap between them and their child.

The individual who has sold his selfhood for easy answers and acceptance by others needs to be brought out of his trance as well. How does a Christian counselor wake this person? First, the counselor wins the person's attention by listening attentively. The counselor responds in a way that indicates concern and support. What the counselor consciously tries to do is offer the friend a basis for an alternate autobiography—one that places control in the hands of the friend and reduces the sense that he or she is a victim of circumstance whose life cannot be brought back under control.

Where there are tensions between individuals and the counselor is a third party, the counselor can accomplish his or her goal when each party is able to communicate with and be heard by the other party. Often the counselor's role is buffer, translator, and megaphone. The counselor accepts the cliches, jargon, preconceptions, and prejudices of one party and reformulates them in the language of the other party. Whenever the counselor detects an unwillingness to listen, the counselor repeats, rephrases, and reasserts the position of the unheard party until the communication is acknowledged. In the process, the counselor absorbs and deflects a considerable amount of disrespect, cynicism, and hostility.

The counselor presents his or her version of the truth and describes the relationship of the family and the individual as the counselor sees it. The counselor articulates the choices that may be made. The counselor offers a picture of a hopeful future without dependencies. And, hopefully, the counselor provides a perspective drawn from who he or she is that will enable the friend to reevaluate his or her experience and relationship with loved ones. The counselor promises continuing interest and support. No matter what the immediate outcome may be, the counselor attempts to leave the door open to further dialogue. And, then, hopeful that all parties are awake and alert to what is really happening and what the options are, the counselor withdraws.

GUIDELINES FOR COUNSELORS

In general, the counselor may adopt one of two strategies: (1) giving advice or (2) fostering transformation. Through giving advice, the counselor is God's instrument, giving comfort and bringing resolution. Giving advice is a skill that requires sensitivity, tact, and the observance of fundamental rules, but it is often just the beginning. Transforming situations from evil to good and changing persons from directionless to self-actualizing requires greater expertise and deeper involvement than giving advice. Both the counselor's advice and his role as an agent of transformation are vital.

RULES FOR GIVING ADVICE

1. *Listen to what is being said.* The effective counselor is, first and foremost, an attentive listener. More counseling is done with the ears than with the mouth.

2. *Consider what is not being said.* Distressed individuals often hide what they really feel behind what they say. Some people have a talent for concealing their deepest emotions behind smoke screens of apparent self-disclosure. Look for the signs—facial expression and posture that do not match the emotional tone of what is being said, frequent hesitation, and avoidance of the real issue.

3. *Ask.* Before advising anyone, be sure that you know what the problem is. If pieces of the puzzle are missing, find out why.

4. *Listen again.* Play dumb. Have your friend repeat the story.

5. *Get the picture—the clear picture, the entire picture.* Don't jump to conclusions. When I was in South Africa, my host warned me about various poisonous snakes—cobras and mambas. If a coil of rope had been left in my closet, I could have misperceived it as a reptile and scared myself to death. Carefully distinguish between coiled ropes (the facts of your friend's situation) and cobras (your presuppositions, prejudices, and possible misinterpretations). Your hasty misreading of your friend's problem can harm both of you.

6. *Restate what you think you have heard.* Make no assumptions. Your friend may be agreeing with your mistaken perceptions of the situation just to please you,

to ensure your continuing attention, or to get you off his back. Remember that neither circumstances nor what people tell you is ever as clear as it seems. As established by Abbott and Costello in their classic dialogue, "Who's on first?" verbal communication is subject to misinterpretation. Further, memory is unreliable; common sense isn't all that common; and you cannot establish what is so by speculating about it.

7. *Prevent defensiveness.* Don't attack, argue, or judge. Your job, at this point, is to sympathize and clarify. Prevent defensiveness by using "I" statements: "I think you are saying— Am I understanding you correctly? I could be wrong but I think what you mean is— Here is what I hear. Is this what you are saying? Is this what you want? Really?

8. *Share who you are.* Express what you believe, how you have triumphed over similar adversities, what lessons you have learned, how your life has been changed. Never be reluctant to cite analogies and parallels from your own experience. I often remember the stories that friends tell me long after I have forgotten their advice. The stories have their point and influence me for years. Personal anecdotes are powerful. They create a sense of community between the parties. The person who is told the story realizes that his adviser is a human being with problems like his.

Don't overdo it. You are supposed to be advising— not performing a one-person show. Stick to the point.

9. *Offer solutions, resolutions as you see them.* People who find themselves in confusing or ambiguous situations want to be told what to do—even when they resist the advice they receive. Decide whether you want to (a) understand and sympathize or (b) negotiate a solution.

10. *Prioritize, help define the steps.* Encourage your friend to develop a definite, time-limited plan of action.

Help assess the resources. Make sure difficulties are not ignored. Respond honestly and critically to the proposed solution.

11. *Negotiate your role (if any).* Are you prepared to help? Are you part of the solution?

Don't feel that you have to say anything. There are times when not giving advice is a more effective form of counseling than giving advice.

12. *Keep your word, follow up.* Set a day and time for reviewing progress on the plan. If you have accepted a role in the plan, schedule a beginning and an end for your involvement.

13. *Predict success.* In the most complete and concrete terms possible, help your friend visualize the attainment of his or her goal. State positively and enthusiastically your faith in his or her ability to accomplish the planned action.

14. *Get out of the way.* Everyone has the right to make his or her own mistakes. The only guarantee for any plan is that there is no guarantee.

SETTING SOME LIMITS

Are there limits to what a concerned individual can do for a friend or neighbor? Yes, indeed. Knowing what cannot be done is just as important as knowing what can be done. Here are some definite "don'ts" for Christians who counsel.

1. *Don't give legal advice.* That's what lawyers do.

2. *Don't play doctor (or pharmacist).* Don't ever try to solve someone's problem by lending them prescription medication such as tranquilizers that your physician originally prescribed for you or for a member of your family. Don't recommend changes in diet or demanding forms of exercise without insisting that your friend receive competent medical advice.

3. *Don't play bank.* Don't lend money to or borrow money from someone you are counseling and limit your generosity to the small gift that indicates your friendship and concern.

4. *Don't solve another's problem by solving yours.* Be responsible and dependable, but take no captives. Don't allow anyone to become dependent on you, no matter how good it makes you feel. Don't become romantically or sexually involved with someone whom you are counseling. Romantic love and intimacy have their place, but they are incompatible with the role of counselor. Be generous with your reassuring smiles, hugs, and pats on the back, but keep it friendly.

Beware of the "victim game." It's played like this: Mary is an abused wife; you encourage her to do what she really wants, to leave her husband; she is grateful to you; she becomes dependent on you; she asks you to solve all her problems; she takes your advice, but finds that she still has problems; she blames you; she begins to feel that you are abusing her just as her husband did. Congratulations. You have progressed from counselor to savior to victimizer.

5. *Don't get in over your head.* You cannot help everyone with every problem. Such patterns of behavior as spouse beating, child abuse, incest, compulsive gambling, drug abuse, and alcoholism require expert intervention. Some disorders in the way people think and perceive the world, such as hearing voices, seeing things that aren't there, constantly suspecting everyone of plotting against them, require the services of a specially trained professional. If a friend of yours becomes suicidal, violent or becomes incapable of providing for basic needs—food, shelter, and clothing—seek a referral from your county's office of social services or mental health services. Encourage your friend to make an appointment or if the situation

requires it, make an appointment for the friend and see that she or he gets there. Your ongoing, compassionate commitment to your friend can be of enormous assistance to those who are rendering professional services on his or her behalf, but don't take it upon yourself to do their job. If your neighbor's roof caught on fire, would you try to put out the conflagration with a seltzer bottle? No. You would phone the fire department!

I think that in our departmentalized, compartmentalized, professionalized society, we are often too eager to call in the police, the courts, and the psychiatrists to deal with difficult people and frustrating problems. But if your gut feeling is that professional intervention is necessary, don't be embarrassed to recommend it. In matters of life or death, get such help immediately.

6. *Don't think that you can love everyone.* Maybe Will Rogers was telling the truth when he said he never met a man he didn't like. But some of them must have sorely tested him! Certain people are like exclusive country clubs, they are not open to everyone. You could be the most loving and competent counselor in your state, but if you remind your neighbor of his first wife or a teacher who failed him in high school, guess what?

7. *Don't expect to succeed every time you try to help someone.* From a common sense standpoint, even Jesus was a failure. Most of his hearers including his friends, spurned his advice. He tried helping us and we killed him. The lesson for the Christian counselor is: Do the best you can and leave it to God to accomplish his purpose *in, through, and in spite* of you.

8. *Don't be discouraged.* The smallest acts of kindness are like the proverbial mustard seed. They come to fruition perennially long after the sower has passed from the scene.

9. *Don't repeat anything told you in confidence except what is required to save a person's life.* Knowing somebody's secrets is a kind of power. It can make you giddy, and the temptation to let a third party know how powerful you are is sometimes irresistible. Also, it is easy to use your concern for your friend as an excuse to "share" and "pray about" what you know with someone who is also concerned. Don't do it. Your "sharing" is just plain gossiping. It will destroy your effectiveness as a counselor and your integrity as a person.

10. *Don't expect to be thanked and don't expect everyone to love you.* A lot of people won't want to hear what you have to say because they don't want to change. That's how they got into difficulty in the first place.

11. *Don't give advice unless you are asked, or unless your advice flows naturally from your relationship with the person to whom the advice is given.* Some people are infinitely warm, supportive, and understanding, but simply cannot tell another person how to live his or her life. Being there for a distressed person—showing interest and concern, being a good listener—is what counts most.

CHAPTER 6

The Counselor as an Agent of Transformation

The scorpion asked the turtle to ford him across a stream. "I don't trust you," said the turtle. "You'll sting me."

"Now why would I do that?" protested the scorpion. "You would die and sink, and I would drown."

Convinced by the scorpion's logic, the turtle took him on his back and began swimming across the stream. In the very middle, the scorpion sank his stinger into the startled turtle's neck. "Why did you do that?" the dying turtle gasped as he sank beneath the surface of the water.

The drowning scorpion replied, "Because it is my nature!"

It is possible for people to change? When it comes to basic character and personality traits, not as much as we would like to think. Dramatic changes in attitudes and behavior are not as common in real life as they are on television. For the most part, shy people stay shy, loud people remain loud, dependent people exchange one dependence for another, people who think the rules apply to everyone but themselves keep breaking the rules, and so forth. As frustrating as it may be, the counselor has to take people as they are, respond to them as openly and compassionately as possible, and leave the result between them and God.

ELEMENTS OF PERSONAL TRANSFORMATION

On rare occasions, I have witnessed alterations in behavior that were so startling, real, and thoroughly convincing that they struck me with awe. It was as though in the twinkling of an eye, character has been transformed; maturity attained; humaneness achieved. Sometimes these conversions were spiritual, and sometimes notion of God, the Bible, and religion had nothing to do with them. Sometimes the magic has lasted and sometimes it has not. Through an examination of thousands of instances of personal transformation, I have learned that certain elements are always present when successful, permanent change occurs. These elements are: self-dissatisfaction, a desire for change, proper conditions, a plan, a new self-image, new patterns of behavior, the support of others, role models, faith in a higher power, persistence, willingness to evaluate and revise a plan, a sense of humor, and a vision of a hopeful future.

Giving advice is one thing; empowering a person to change is another. Giving advice is like a putting an adhesive bandage on a scraped knee. It is a response to an immediate problem. Much more demanding than giving advice is the task of motivating others to transform not only the conditions of their lives but their lives themselves. Is it possible to stimulate change in another person? Yes. Agents of change ranging from AA and Amway to self-help seminars and television evangelists do it all the time. What such agents have in common is that they first change behavior, that changes in behavior elicit changes in attitudes, that changes in attitudes produce changes in beliefs, and, finally, that changes in beliefs lead to changes in personal feelings. There is a technology of personal transformation that can be used to help those whom we counsel to articulate and achieve their desires for personal development. Enhancing individuals' freedom requires that we enable them to liberate themselves from old scripts, discredited beliefs, self-destructive patterns of behavior, undesirable automatic or mechanistic forces, negative self-images, and whatever else binds them to the hurts, narrowness, and smallness of the past. What I am suggesting is that the counselor, with the permission and active participation of his or her friend, take charge and create an appropriate atmosphere for self-transformation.

The job of the counselor is to enhance the ability of the friend to choose responsibly; that is, to determine what he or she wants, to determine how to get it, and, then, to get it. Counseling is the process of stimulating the ability of another to transform his or her situation from undesirable to desirable. It is the process of realistically defining what one wants and how to obtain it, of assessing the cost, and deciding whether one is willing to pay it.

1. *Developing a wish list.* The first step is helping individuals express what they really want. Ask. Write down the answers. And ask again. Don't be afraid to make suggestions. You may be more aware of what your friends really want than they are. Ask them whom they admire, and why. Encourage them to describe in as concrete terms as possible what they would consider a perfect day in their life. Ask them to recall some of the happiest times in their past and use them as part of their image of an ideal day.

I have discovered that many of my clients suffer from a lack of desire. They have no concrete want list. They do not feel that they deserve anything, so why should they have desires? The stimulation of desire is powerful in ungluing individuals from a state of depression, lethargy, and dependence. Free persons know what they want. Until individuals develop an acute sense of goals, hopes, and dreams, they will remain stuck.

2. *Creating proper conditions.* The next step is creating the proper conditions. Change requires an appropriate setting, a time and a place especially chosen for the purpose. Change is rarely undertaken in the midst of one's hectic and harried everyday life. Arrange for an undisturbed time—at least two hours—to spend alone with your friend to discuss the changes he or she desires and your mutual plan for attaining them. Encourage your friend to devote at least forty-five minutes a day for at least twenty-one consecutive days to the pursuit of these goals.

3. *Articulating faith.* Consciously and unconsciously, individuals must feel that the world they live in or the spiritual reality that underlies that world fundamentally supports their struggle for a new life. The attainment of one's own wishes requires a sense of a moral order that rewards virtue, persistence, and honesty. I am not dictating a list of mandatory beliefs or ethical dos and don'ts. What I am suggesting is that you ask your friend to write out answers to the following questions: What kind of world do I want? As I pursue what I want, what must be true of reality in order for me to get it? At this point, individuals must develop their own list of moral or theological certainties about themselves, their dealings with others, and the order of things.

The counselor should promote the articulation by the subject of what the counselor believes about God and the world. The counselor should urge the friend, for the sake of the experiment in self-transformation, to live for the next month as if there were a caring God who supported the struggles of the individual, as if living according to one's highest values would be rewarded and deviation from these values would be punished, and as if the universe responded to all efforts at self-transformation with approval and support.

I tell my clients that each of us should be our own theologian and ethicist, elaborating our own systems of truths. There are many paradigms available from religious thinkers, preachers, the scriptures of the world's religions, the faith of our childhood, philosophers, novelists, poets, motivational and self-help writers. There is no need to reinvent the wheel; we only need to install it.

The counselor can appeal to his or her own cherished beliefs. An individual who is eager to change is open to hear what has brought satisfaction to the life of the one who is advising. Do not be shy about sharing your faith. And suggest that your friends keep a written record of what they believe and how their own system of faith develops as they progress. (Keep a diary of your own. It is amazing how vivid and exciting one's previously taken-for-granted faith becomes when one articulates it for the sake of another.)

4. *Nurturing the child.* The counselor should nourish the friend's child-nature. Within each of us is a frightened, bewildered five-year-old child who is eager to play and desirous only of acceptance. Encourage your friend to indulge occasionally in non-utilitarian play activities. Activities that are "just for fun" enable one to suspend judgment, accept oneself and others, and lower barriers to self-knowledge and intimacy. As a counselor, I encourage my clients to bombard themselves with the enjoyment of their emerging selves. Encourage your friends to imagine that they are taking care of and enjoying the company of the love-starved five-year-old within. Have them award themselves with tokens of self-approval, such as gold stars or special

treats, as they progress. From time to time, I have given my "five-year-old" a marionette, a wooden train, kazoos, and a Mickey Mouse telephone. This may sound childish, but the point is to reach the neglected and abused child in each of us. Scrooge's Christmas morning antics were definitely infantile; they were also redemptive.

5. *Changing self-image.* One's self-image may be regarded as a product of circumstances and fate, about which nothing can be done or as a creation that incorporates what is given by circumstances with what is conceived by the individual. In order to stop taking the victim's position in life, it is necessary to accept responsibility for one's self-image.

All achievement has as its source an idea freely created. Before the building of any invention is the conception of that invention. Before the writing of any novel is the imagining of that novel. Ideas have an inherent tendency to transform themselves into reality. The more tangible and concrete the idea is, the more likely that it will be realized. If you want to motivate a man to earn a million dollars, put him in a room with ten thousand hundred dollar bills piled on a table. Lock the door and leave him there alone with the money for an hour. The real million dollars will inflame his imagination much more than somebody else's words about a million dollars. Likewise, giving deliberate and regular attention to well-elaborated, focused, and specific images of the self will tend to transform these images into reality.

An individual can only think of one thing at a time and can only think in the present. What one chooses to think can influence the future. Each thought is the beginning of a causal chain that determines the direction of every moment that follows. Our attitudes and our beliefs limit and channel our experiences. As

Louise L. Hay observes in her recorded study course, *You Can Heal Your Life* (Farmingdale, N.Y.: Coleman Publishing, 1985), "The point of power is always in the present moment." Each moment is a new beginning. One's current thought is the only thing over which one has any control. And what one is thinking here and now creates one's tomorrow.

Positive images and expectations open the door to opportunities and successes. Resentment, self-criticism, guilt, and fear slam the door shut. Bad ideas force out good ideas, so systematically uproot your friend's negative judgments and self-criticisms. Negative ideas interfere with positive ideas and with positive self-expectations. An essential part of creating a positive self-image begins with avoiding resentment, self-righteousness, and guilt. Such states fasten us to the past, prevent us from dealing with the present, and cause dissatisfaction. The past has no power over us. What has happened has happened. We cannot change it.

There are three ways to deal with the past: (1) we can blame others for yesterday's evils and allow ourselves to be overcome with sadness, anger, and regret; (2) we can deride ourselves for our past blunders and determine that we will not repeat our mistakes in the future; and (3) we can forgive those who harmed us in the past, realizing that they were as much victims as we were, and forgive ourselves as well. The first and second choices cement us in the past. The third releases us to be, do, and achieve.

Resentment, self-righteousness, and guilt create inhibition. Encourage your friends to choose to be free right here and now, to avoid the victim's game and to accept responsibility for their thoughts, their actions, their feelings, their expectations. Help them focus their thoughts on who they are, what they are capable of being, on those present aspects of their character and personality that they and others genuinely admire. Urge your friends to fight their way through their inhibitions, to do what they want to do despite their reticence, shyness, and fear of rejection. And praise each success—no matter how inconsequential it may seem. For success leads to success.

Through techniques of active imagination, help your friend recreate expectations, and, hence, influence everyday reality. Have your friend create a positive self-image by (a) placing himself or herself in a state of physical relaxation and (b) actively, concretely imagining himself or herself as the new and transformed self. The state of relaxation may be attained by prayer, meditation (e.g., focusing on one's breathing while counting the breaths), "relaxation response" (the successive, intentional tightening and relaxing of the muscles in each part of the body), chanting, listening to calming music, taking a hot bath, walking in nature, flooding one's consciousness with pleasant memories— whatever works for a given individual.

Maxwell Maltz suggests in *Psycho-Cybernetics* that we retreat into "a room of the mind" for at least thirty minutes a day. He urges us to imagine in vivid detail that we possess everything we want—objects, relationships, honors, learning. His conviction is that the nervous system cannot distinguish between an actual experience and one vividly imagined.

In *You Can Heal Your Life,* Louise L. Hay teaches that after one has thoroughly concentrated on draining the tension from each part of the body, physical relaxation should be enhanced with the recitation of the following affirmation:

I am willing to let go;
I release;
I relax;
I release fear; I release anger; I release guilt; I release
sadness; I release limitations;
I am at peace;
I am safe;
I am me; it is safe to be me;
I let go and I am at peace.

The period of relaxation and the practice of active
visualization must be regular and consistent—at least
twenty minutes a day for three weeks. Maltz maintains
that it takes twenty-one days for a new suggestion or
positive self-image to take hold. I find it significant that
most self-help and conversionist sect groups observe a
twenty-one to forty-day period of indoctrination or
advanced studies. They seem to know what Maltz has
observed, that three weeks of concrete visualization of a
new identity while in a relaxed or altered state enables
the new suggestion to take hold in the individual's
unconscious mind.

6. *Creating community.* Active imagination is greatly
enhanced by surrounding oneself with supportive
friends and acquaintances. Napoleon Hill, Martin
Buber, Dale Carnegie, and Werner Erhard are acutely
aware of the importance of the individual's involvement
in an ongoing mutual support group. Like all new ideas,
an enhanced self-image requires confirmation. It must
be articulated in an appropriate language, acted out in
accepted forms of behavior, and take root in transformed attitudes—all of which require the support of
others in a community of like concerns. The weakness
of most forms of self-help therapy and motivational
philosophy is that it pays scant attention to the social
aspect. Transformation requires the encouragement of
others. Moreover, change is fostered by role models,

exemplars, and paradigms, who have already struggled and won.

Recommend that your friends create their own community. Unless there is an ongoing experience of others who share and live by the values that the changed individual has accepted, change will eventually wear off. For without support, deliberation fades and good intentions are forgotten. Suggest that they deliberately surround themselves with persons who reinforce their most hopeful, creative moments and who experience themselves as supportive of theirs. And propose that they withdraw from persons and circumstances that needlessly depress, suppress, limit, restrict, or inhibit them. Remind them to listen to their own thoughts, monitor their own responses. If they start becoming unduly self-critical, remind them that negativity is a bad habit. Urge them to let go of guilt, resentment, and self-righteousness—not by resisting them but by replacing them with positive alternatives.

7. *Changing patterns of behavior.* As your friends change their self-image, they must also change their patterns of behavior. Getting what we want requires that we plan for it by setting goals, assessing resources, developing strategies, scheduling our time, and evaluating our progress. The style or format of setting goals and monitoring progress is relatively unimportant as long as there is a conscious, deliberate, and articulated process.

The counselor might suggest to those who wish to adopt a technology of self-transformation: Change your pattern of behavior—dress differently, get a new haircut, attend the early church service for the next few Sundays instead of the late service (or the late service instead of the early), pursue a neglected hobby, read a book that you have never found time for or see a movie that you missed in your youth (video-cassette recorders and tapes of movies are available for rental in most communities). Take a college course dealing with something that has always interested you. Do a dozen things that you desire and value. Those actions will generate attitudes, beliefs, and feelings that will support your enhanced self-image.

8. *Planning and persistence.*   However, desiring success and planning for it are useless without persistence. The results of everything that has been urged to this point must constantly be fed back into the visualization and self-imaging process.

Insist that your friend put his or her faith into action. When I "graduate" my clients from self-transformation counseling, I tell them something like this:

> *If you believe something, share that belief. Support the hopes of others. Involve yourself in your community. Apply your faith to the real issues of our times—however you define them. Above all, keep your word. For the failure of individuals, groups, businesses, and government to honor their promises is the most destructive force at work in our society today. Conversely, a restoration of a sense of honor and commitment—doing what you have said you would—is the surest hope for your own well-being or for the sanity of your world. Live as if each act is important. For it either expresses the purpose for which you live or it reveals the emptiness of your existence. The choice is yours to make. And that is, after all, the meaning of freedom.*

Help your friends plan, promote, and persevere in their plans. Remind them that even the most miraculous conversion requires a step-by-step program for anchoring the changes in the individual's everyday life—including their family, work, and interpersonal relations. Set a special time to evaluate their progress in concrete terms, refine, replan, and go on.

About three weeks into the process, individuals should be encouraged to ask themselves: Is it all really worth it? Do I still want what I set out to achieve? For they must constantly renew their sense of what they want, what they value, and their realization that they have taken charge, have accepted responsibility for their own self-image, their own life.

9. *Humor and reinforcement.* And during the entire process, keep your sense of humor so that your friend may keep his or hers. The ability to laugh at one's foibles and excesses probably frees a person from more mistakes than all the sermons ever preached. If you can maintain a sense of perspective, so will your friend.

Constant positive reinforcement is extremely important. Affirm that you believe in your friends and their plans. Stress their progress. Compliment them when they self-correct along the way. Show as much affection and approval as you can comfortably give. More encouragement is given by friendly hugs than by bouquets of flowers. And remember that predictions of success have a way of fulfilling themselves. When someone the individual respects predicts that change is possible, is happening, will continue to happen and that there is a hopeful future, the individual's change is confirmed and supported. Without it, progress is uncertain.

Each of us has a tendency to obey those who remind us of our inner parent figure and to conform to the expectations of those who accept and love us. The self-training program that we recommend encourages a unique form of obedience and conformity. It challenges individuals to be their own parents and their own peers and to accept responsibility for their own self-image and for the world they choose to live in. Of course, it is easier to drift from one immediate satisfaction to the next with no goals. Or to allow an organized, manipulative group or a designing individual to seduce, indoctrinate, and control us. The processes that we have sketched require discipline, persistence, and imagination. They demand an awareness and a responsiveness on the part of the counselor as well as by the counselor's friend which may prove positively taxing.

There are no easy roads to self-transformation. Discovering and enjoying one's freedom is not a comfortable path. As a counselor, I daily remind myself that only the truth that I find for myself through my own struggle with anxiety, pain, and uncertainty can set me free. And whatever my role may be as an enabler, only the truth that my friends and clients accept and actualize for themselves can enrich their lives.

CHAPTER 7

More Advice to Counselors

Case Notes: *Richard*

Richard, a friend of mine, describes his involvement in a church youth group thirty years ago:

John, a senior at a local seminary, was the youth director at our church and I was a sixteen-year-old novice Christian, who had been elected president of the group. We spent a great deal of time together, planning programs, studying the Bible, and praying. We became close friends and trusted each other. I told him about my frustrations and confusions, and he told me about the sexual sins of several members of the youth group. At first, I felt honored that he would share such "adult" matters with me. Then, I realized that he was violating the confidences of the other members of the group, coloring his reminiscences of their confessions for his own voyeuristic enjoyment, and that he was prejudicing my attitudes toward my peers. It dawned on me that if he violated my friends' confidences to impress me, there was nothing that would stop him from sharing my confidences with them.

I quit the group. I heard a few months later that he was telling my former friends that I had left because my girl friend was pregnant, which was not true. It was many years before I would trust anyone with confidences about my personal life.

A THORN IN THE FLESH

The term "thorn in the flesh" has found its way from a letter by the Apostle Paul into vernacular English. In his second letter to them, Paul discloses to his spiritual children at Corinth: "So to prevent me from being overly elated, there was given to me a thorn in the flesh, a messenger of Satan so that he might beat me up so that I should not be overly elated" (II Cor. 12:7 LDS).

Paul had brought the gospel of Christ Jesus to the Corinthians and now they questioned his authority. They had turned to false apostles, to "peddlers of God's word." They had learned to receive but not to give. They had learned to accept forgiveness but not how to repent. And, above all they had not learned appreciation.

What was Paul's thorn in the flesh? An eye condition? In his letter to the Galatians, he recalls that he had suffered from "a bodily ailment" when he first preached to them, and that they would have plucked out their own eyes and given them to him (4:13-16). Epilepsy? Some commentators have maintained that the accounts of his conversion experience sound suspiciously like descriptions of epileptic seizures.

Or was it simply lack of appreciation?

It is so much easier to criticize, scandalize, and gossip; to bring greatness down to our level; to find feet of clay. When I was a young man, most of my relationships were based on mutual misery. For example, in graduate school my friends and I would denigrate our professors and somehow feel that the human feelings of "great men" made them no better than us neophytes. Our currency, our medium of exchange, was gossip. I will tell you some secret about so and so whom you respect, that is *fear and resent,* and you will give me some juicy morsel in return.

And behind our failure to appreciate others was our lack of respect for ourselves. We did not realize or appreciate who we were in ourselves, in relationship to others, or in Christ, and so we engaged in the no-win game of devaluation. Here is how it is played:

I will believe anyone who says I am average and no one who says that I am special.

I will believe anyone who says that another is below average and no one who says that another is special.

I will believe anyone who says that a great person is unimpressive and no one who says that a great person is outstanding.

I will be content with the lowest common denominator because that excuses my being average or less than average.

If anyone renders a service to me, I will devalue it. If I devalue the service (or the servant), I will not be obligated to show appreciation, pay my bill, act with civility.

If anyone loves me, I will devalue both the love and the one who loves. If I devalue the object of my love and devotion, I will not be obligated to be faithful or to honor my commitment.

If I accomplish anything, I will devalue it. If I devalue myself, I will not be obligated to keep my word. If I do not keep my word, nothing will be expected of me.

The devaluation game must be extremely popular. I seldom meet anyone with exaggerated self-esteem or a superiority complex. To say that a client or friend has low self-esteem is similar to saying he is alive.

The devaluation game is incompatible with counseling. If you feel tempted to play, find some place other than counseling to deal with your low self-esteem and your need to bring others down to your own level. Find a counselor of your own! When you counsel others, they will trust you with confidences, confess sins and shortcomings, burden you with dark thoughts and secret fears. As a friend and counselor, you must renounce the right to repeat without permission one word that you have heard. Counseling is serious business. There is no place for gossip. And by the same token, never trust a gossip or anyone who enters into relationship with you based on their breaking their word to a third party. If a person will gossip with you, he or she will gossip about you. If he or she will violate the trust of another to tell you a juicy secret, he or she will surely not keep the secrets that you convey "in strictest confidence."

Perhaps Paul's thorn in the flesh was that he knew he was "Paul the apostle," the messenger and agent of God, the one sent and empowered to bring the world to Christ. He knew that he was elite and elect, that he was totally non-interchangeable, in no way average. He respected himself for who he was. What a burden to bear!

Do you know that you are John the apostle, or Mary the apostle, or Henry the apostle, or Mandy the apostle, or Keith the apostle, or (fill in your own name) the apostle? As a counselor, can you accept your special calling and help others realize theirs?

Was it arrogant of Paul to know what cannot really be known at all? Could he prove to anyone that he really was God's messenger of salvation to the Gentiles? He could have considered the alternatives, played it safe, been like everyone else, sat around mending tents in Damascus while he gossiped about the other apostles.

It is so tiresome to hear people's excuses for not being who they could be, for not doing what they feel they ought to be doing, and how everybody else is no good. It is uplifting to be with people who spontaneously and unapologetically do whatever they do from a sense of who they are, what their vocation is, and what their election and eliteness in Christ are—even if their eliteness is being chosen to live a quiet, normal, ordinary existence.

Moment by moment, Christian counselors must engage in *evaluation, appreciation,* and *thanksgiving.* They must be alert to the possibilities in others that have never before been discovered. They must throw the whole power of their being into empowering others and appreciating what others accomplish. They must thank God for the gifts this evaluation and appreciation give—both to others and to themselves. They must learn to appreciate themselves for the indispensable role they play; for evaluation, appreciation, and thanksgiving are one and the same.

CHAPTER 8

Victims of the Victims of the Victims

Case Notes: *Gordon*

My friend Gordon, a former psychologist who is now a commercial artist, has taught me as much about counseling as anyone I have ever known. Recently, he was telling me about his experiences as a client of professional therapists. What he says is so significant that I would like to devote the next few pages to his story.

The first time I sought help was when I developed a terrible case of writer's block trying to start the first draft of my doctoral dissertation. It had taken me two years to get a proposal approved. First, I would send the committee an outline, and about three months later they would send it back with suggested revisions. So I would rewrite it, making several phone calls along the way to my major adviser to try to figure out what was really wanted. It would take me about two months to send the committee a new proposal. And then I'd wait three months for the next response. It was demoralizing, and what they seemed to want was getting further and further from anything that interested me. When I finally got approval, I became depressed and paralyzed. I just knew that nothing I wrote would please them, so I went to see a therapist.

For several months we talked about my childhood. I had always felt anger toward my mother, who I remembered as being quite abusive. You know, mostly verbal stuff like, "What's wrong with you? Why are you such a slob? Why can't you keep your room clean? You'll never get into a good college with your grades. Why do you date such mediocre girls?" Also she was pretty free with an electrical cord. Maybe she only beat me and my younger sister three or four times, but that's how I always remember her—totally out of control and coming after us with that cord.

Anyway, the therapist told me that we always fail to identify our problem parent and that my real problem was with my father. The therapist said that my father had been competing with me for my mother's attention since the day I was born and that my depression was caused by my feeling that I would never be as good as my dad. After all, when I was a kid, he was always stronger and smarter. So according to the therapist, I was reacting to my major adviser as though he were my disapproving father.

This "realization" did nothing to remove my writer's block. It just made me terrifically angry with my father. I didn't speak to him for years.

After about ten visits, the therapist became impatient with me as we ended a session. He told me not to try to write anything until our next visit, which would be in three weeks because he was going on vacation. He said that I should do whatever I could to entertain myself—go to the movies, attend concerts, read poetry—whatever I felt like doing, but that I was not to write one single word. He said that there was an important therapeutic reason, which he would explain the next time he saw me.

So for two weeks, I did as instructed. I phoned long-lost old friends. I went to the zoo and the art museums. I read some novels. I visited antique stores in the country. I went clothes shopping. I took my daughter to a dairy farm where ice cream is made, and we had two hot fudge sundaes—each! These were all things that I had neglected for three years while in graduate school.

After two weeks, I was writing a letter one day. I rolled a sheet of paper into my electric typewriter, and, almost without thinking about what I was doing, I wrote the first page of the introduction to my dissertation. When I realized what I was doing, I felt guilty. After all, I was paying my therapist for his advice, and I was not following it. The next day, I decided that what I really wanted to do that day was write, so I wrote the next ten pages of the introduction.

By the time of my next appointment with the therapist, I was off to a running start. I told him, and he was pleased. Then I asked him what the therapeutic reason for his advice was. "What advice?" he asked. "The advice that I not try to write for three weeks," I explained. "I thought you were trying to illustrate 'paradoxical intentionality,' " I added. He didn't know what I was talking about.

The next time I saw a counselor was about five years later. It was because I was very anxious and depressed as the result of the stresses of my work as a counselor of abused children. I went to see this psychiatrist for whom I had tremendous respect. He said, "Of course, you are upset. You have an upsetting job!" He shared with me some of his own reactions to the kind of family problems I was trying to help people with. I had been counseling for three years, and he for twenty-five. Hearing about the times he had wanted to quit, how trapped he felt by his training and the expectations of the community, and so on, was liberating.

A year later, my job was getting to me again, so I went to see this social worker. We went through my childhood once more. She tried to convince me that my problems stemmed from the lousy job of parenting my folks had done. They had given me an unsatisfactory "life script." And I became enraged with both of them. I have to admit,

I gave them a pretty hard time the next time they visited me, but that didn't make me feel any better.

I was talking to my younger sister one day about our childhood. It turned out that she had her share of bitter memories. She was even angry with me for the way certain things I had done had affected her. "When you were at college and Mom and Dad got angry with you, they used to fight with each other—each of them blaming the other for the fact that you weren't interested in anything practical, anything that would make money, and that you decided to marry someone they couldn't stand. Sometimes they would argue all night and Mom would threaten to leave Dad. Their fights made me feel as if there was nothing safe and secure in my life. I was mad at you. It was all your fault." It seemed silly to me. I had never intended to make her feel insecure.

My sister said that I should try to understand how it must have been for Mom and Dad. They grew up during the Depression, so financial security was important to them. The only thing they ever heard from their parents was "get an education"; "get a good job"; or "marry someone who has a good job."

As she spoke, I began to wonder what kind of parents my grandparents had had. Then the light bulb went on in my head! I suddenly realized: *"We are all the victims of the victims of the victims."* I remember feeling sadness, compassion, and anger all at the same time. I was genuinely sad about my parents' struggles and sufferings. I understood for the first time in my life why they had put so much pressure on me and my sister to succeed—as they defined success. But I was also angry with them for trying to live their lives through me. And I was angry with myself. I realized that everything I had ever done was either to please them or to get even with them. I was letting myself be their victim and blaming them for my unhappiness. I decided right there and then that I didn't want to think of myself as their victim ever again. I didn't want to live as if I were a victim, as if I had no control over my fate.

I also decided that I did not enjoy being a counselor, and

so I quit. The depression that had hovered around me for so many years lifted like a cloud being burned off by the sunshine.

I probably will never know if I became a therapist because my parents wanted me to be an engineer, or because I wanted to be like Dad and Grampa Earl—both of whom were tremendously supportive and understanding to me at times, or because my high school guidance counselor said that I was a natural counselor. But I know that when I act like the automatic, mechanical effect of some big causal machine, when I sell myself on the notion that I was screwed up by my parents, or the government, or the media, or the birth rate, or the fact that I'm the firstborn son, or that I'm right-handed, or that I'm a Gemini, I just settle into feeling sorry for myself, and I accomplish nothing. When I sense that I'm playing martyr, I just remind myself: *"We are all the victims of the victims of the victims."* And then I ask myself, "So what if we are? Does it make any difference here and now?" And I stop acting like a victim.

All my counseling experiences—my work as a counselor and my having been counseled—have convinced me that human memory is so malleable that it is practically unreliable. When I feel good about myself, I cherish the memories I have of the good times with my parents and sister, of the good times we had together. When I feel sad, I remember the bad things "they did to me." And I wonder if the highs were really as high or the lows really as low as I remember.

When I worked with severely disturbed parents—child abusers and alcoholics—I discovered that their memories of their past always justified their present failings. As children, they were abused themselves by their parents. Their parents were alcoholics, so being alcoholic was the only example they had for being an adult. Agreeing with their interpretations, giving credence to their memories of their own childhood, only seemed to give approval to their present behavior, so many of them didn't want to change.

They didn't want to accept responsibility for their own behavior or for their own happiness. They just wanted to be understood.

I remember this one client who had been convicted of molesting his ten-year-old stepdaughter. "She made me do it," he whined. "She used to swing her hips when she walked away from me, and when she'd look at me she'd lick her lips. She knew what she was doing. She wanted it." Just think, I was supposed to feel sorry for him because he was the fifty-year-old stooge of a ten-year-old seductress. He believed that *he* was the victim!

So what lessons can we draw from Gordon's experiences as a client and as a counselor?

1. *Don't play the victim game.* The kind of counseling I am recommending in these pages is based on responding to the here and now.

An anxious or troubled person is easily influenced by someone else's explanation of why he or she is anxious or troubled. Simply hearing our own story as told by some objective third party relieves a remarkable amount of the distress. We are particularly prone to believe stories that assign the responsibility for our unhappiness to persons, influences, sources, causes, factors over which we have no control. The past is the surest refuge. It is apparently beyond anyone's control. Notice I say "apparently." As Gordon informs us, memory is plastic; it conveniently conforms to our need to be victims.

When a person you are counseling starts blaming another person or circumstances for what is wrong with his or her life, take it with a ton of salt. Memory is not a tape recorder; it is a creative process. That's why the courts are suspicious of memories that are enhanced by hypnosis or lie detector tests. Facts are invented, distorted, and falsified even by those who have no intention of deceiving anyone.

Don't argue. Listen carefully to your friend's complaints. Then tactfully ask your friend to answer one question about the tormenters: Whose victims are they? Of whom are *they* the victims? And remind your friend that blaming others will not solve his or her problems.

Finally, encourage your friend to file the blame away in a mental cabinet marked "for future consideration." Or have your friend write all the sad, angry, resentful memories on lined notebook paper. Then, instruct him or her to tear the paper into pieces, burn the pieces, and flush the ashes down the nearest toilet.

2. *Don't time travel.* Stay in the present. What is happening now? And what can be done about today? Steer your friends away from the past. Encourage them to be alert to what they are doing with their lives, where they want to go, and what they want to do. The sense of a hopeful future can only be built on a willingness to take control of one's own life, to accept responsibility, to assess resources, to define needs, to plan, and, ultimately, to do.

3. *Share your own accomplishments, successes, and breakthroughs.* Success is contagious. Gordon received more help from the psychiatrist who recounted his struggles and accomplishments as a therapist than he did from months of reconstructing his childhood. For the most part, major change is facilitated by one's inner images of heroes, examples, and role models.

As the legends and myths of every civilization make plain, human beings identify with those who have overcome adversity and prospered. Sir Edmund Hillary, when asked why he wanted to climb Mt. Everest, said, "Because it's there!" But he might as well have said, "Because it's there just as other previously unclimbed high mountains were there before it, and I know the men who climbed them." A few heroes are born; some are hoaxes invented by public relations; but most are self-created out of the expectations, encouragement, and examples of others.

4. *When doing nothing is the best thing to do, suggest that your friend do nothing.* Sometimes the very attempt to solve a problem is what is keeping the problem from being solved.

If I were to set off a firecracker at your feet and then tell you that you had to recite the Gettysburg Address within one minute, you might be more worried about the next firecracker than about the recitation. The harder you try, the harder the job becomes.

If I were inadvertently to drop a piece of a jigsaw puzzle on the floor and spend several hours trying to complete the puzzle, I would not be able to—no matter how many times I tried.

I get very impatient with colleagues who think that if half a job can be done in eight consecutive hours, the whole job can be finished in sixteen straight. No way. At some point, fatigue sets in and a person begins redoing or undoing what he or she has done.

Leave the puzzle on the table overnight. You will find the pieces instantly when you again return to it. Unless your project is the kind that can be completely finished in an extra ten minutes but would take hours to restart later, don't hesitate to quit and return to it when you have a clear head.

As a counselor, constantly remind yourself that about half of all creative work and problem solving is done unconsciously. Pack the conscious mind with as much data as you can and allow it to percolate. Leaving a problem unsolved and deliberately trying not to solve a problem are important parts of the creative process. When Gordon left his futile efforts to begin his dissertation and surrendered to self-entertainment and relaxation, his unconscious abilities took over. After all, he had consciously programmed himself to accomplish a goal, and the goal was quite doable given his talent and resources.

After two weeks, the combination of his unconscious abilities and his goal orientation had taken charge. He could no longer *not* write. What the two weeks of self-indulgence had accomplished was a stilling of the distracting mental noise—his self-doubts, fears, memories of past failures.

5. *When the best advice is no advice, give none—just be there.* Gordon's sister did not intentionally attempt to help him deal with his depression. Gordon's first therapist did not seriously intend for him to do nothing for three weeks. (He told Gordon that he had no recollection of having given any such advice. He probably made some offhand suggestion that Gordon might as well go to the movies for all the good the therapy was doing him.) Gordon's sister and his therapist were there when he needed them. In the midst of whatever was transpiring between Gordon and his sister or Gordon and his therapist, Gordon's talking with them allowed him to create for himself a safe, non-threatening, nonjudgmental environment in which he could sort out his thoughts, examine his situation from a fresh vantage point, and discover for himself what he really needed. By listening to himself, he was able to break the emotional stalemate. Some-

times merely being there with and for others without giving a word of advice allows them to send a signal to themselves that it is all right to pay attention to their own needs and to the solutions that are suddenly clear and at hand.

C H A P T E R 9

Anger and Forgiveness

Case Notes: *Frieda*

Frieda, in her mid-thirties, is an office manager. She is married and has two children. During a discussion of forgiveness at a church adult school class, she stated:

When I returned to the church as an adult, nothing bothered me more than Jesus' requirement of forgiveness. I had become so accustomed to blaming others for the terrible things I had suffered, and holding grudges. There is so much anger in me, and it is hard to just let go of it.

I have never forgiven my cousin April, who tried to get me to play sex games with her when I was twelve and she was sixteen. It made me feel so dirty and ashamed. I have not seen her in twelve years, and I don't want to. And there was Mary at work. She lied to the boss and manipulated things so that I lost my job. I was out of work for five months. My new job pays a lot less than the old one did. I've really tried, but I just can't find it in me to forgive April or Mary.

The worst part of not being able to "forgive and forget" is the remembering. When I wake up in the morning, I am arguing in my head with April and Mary. I am telling them the things I wish I had said. Or I am imagining what might have been if I had stood up for myself and not let these things happen to me. Some mornings it takes me two hours to silence the voices.

Karen

Todd Perkins, a minister in New Jersey, was telling me recently about one of his congregants, Karen, a young woman in her late teens. As he related:

Karen and her family have been at odds for six years. She is a real screw-up. Of all the kids in our junior group she has caused the most trouble, demanded the most attention, and made herself the most miserable. She was suspended from high school several times, and has been unable to hold a job. And there have been problems with booze and drugs. Her parents have tried everything—scolding, threatening, punishing, coming to the church for counseling, going with Karen to professional therapists. Nothing seems to help.

She came to see me this morning and she seemed much happier than usual. You might say that she shone. She told me that she had had a major argument with her father the night before. He had been drinking and was using very abusive language. All of a sudden it dawned on her: "This is his crap, not mine. Let him carry it. I don't want any part of it." Karen felt better than she had felt in several years.

DEALING WITH ANGER

Anger is the natural overflow of a person's essential irritability. Each of us has his or her own boiling point. Annoyances do not so much anger us as provide us with an opportunity to express our underlying aggravation. Let's take a hypothetical situation:

My friend Harlan is driving along on the Bayshore Freeway. Traffic is heavy and he is afraid that he will be late for work. Suddenly a car cuts into his lane, forcing him to hit his brakes. Harlan gets angry. He leans on his horn. The driver behind Harlan hits his brakes, leans on his horn, and shouts an unprintable, rude remark.

The driver who cuts in front of Harlan does not *make* him angry; by giving Harlan the choices of either slowing down or running into him, he provides Harlan the excuse to articulate feelings that were just below the surface of his consciousness before the other driver's automobile appeared. When Harlan slows down, he gives an opportunity to the driver behind him to display his feelings by sounding his horn, which, in turn, gives Harlan a new opportunity, which Harlan articulates with an appropriate hand gesture, which gives the driver behind Harlan a new opportunity. In the meantime, the driver behind the driver behind Harlan contributes an expression of his irritability, and in no time there are multiple examples of the natural overflow of the feeling variously known as anger, animosity, hostility, rage, huff, indignation, miff, offense, pique, resentment, frenzy, fury, ire, outrage, tantrum, and wrath!

What is it that keeps the chain reaction of offended drivers from erupting into an explosion of violence and homicide? Only the phenomena of *divergent boiling points* and *dissimilar expressiveness*. No two of us erupt at exactly the same level of provocation, and our responses are as varied as our temperaments and backgrounds. Under most conditions, being cut off on the freeway bothers me; I have a mid-range boiling point. My automatic form of expression when thus annoyed is to talk to the interior of my automobile as though I were addressing the offender: "You stupid idiot! Who taught you how to drive?" I don't sound my horn; I don't make obscene hand gestures, and I don't know why I don't.

At some point in my life, I chose to talk to myself when annoyed by other drivers. It was a form of retaliation consistent with my self-image. Since passengers in my automobile reinforced my selection by agreeing with me and adding their unflattering opinions of the other person, it became a conditioned reflex. Reality itself seemed to further add its approval to my mode of responding by sparing me punishment or retribution for my response.

In a W. C. Fields short subject, "Road Hogs," a well-to-do man and his wife spend their time on the road in a succession of new cars, intentionally inflicting harm to the vehicles of discourteous drivers. (I wonder if this film inspired amusement park "bumper cars"?) If I were to make a motion picture about the same emotion, my response would be more in line with that of Fields, and the malefactor's vehicle would be dissolved by a laser beam. What a delicious fantasy!

The New Testament message is that a human being cannot control the fact that he is angry, but he can choose the form of expression. The automatic form of expression is a learned behavior. Inappropriate responses can be unlearned and replaced with productive ones. In the words of the Apostle Paul: "Be angry but do not sin; do not let the sun go down on your anger. . . . Let all bitterness and wrath and anger and clamor and slander be put away from you, with all malice, and be kind to one another, tenderhearted, forgiving one another, as God in Christ forgave you" (Eph. 4:26, 31-32). Jesus could become highly irritated and could express that anger with words and actions. His critics, enemies, and followers felt the sting of his denunciations, reprimands, and rebukes. The cleansing of the Temple was scarcely an act of nonviolent civil disobedience. For Jesus, anger was an opportunity. His anger energized him to confront issues, demand change, comfort the afflicted, and afflict the comfortable.

Anger is a power, an elemental force. Like all energy it may be used for good or evil. Unleashed and out of control, anger becomes destructive. Channeled and directed, it has the potential for deepening relationships, harmonizing incompatible egos, and building community.

In all real relationships among human beings, anger is inevitable. The repressed rage—the accumulated resentments, hurts, and misunderstandings—lurks in each of us like a starving predator waiting for an opportunity to pounce. Sometimes the reaction is "justified" by the lack of consideration, insensitivity, and rudeness shown to us by the object of our anger. Indeed, there are broken promises and neglected commitments enough to excuse every angry word that any of us will ever utter, or every vindictive deed that we will ever perform. The question is not, Do we have the right to get angry? The question is, Do the "justifications" make our anger appropriate? Or, do we act out our anger because we are fundamentally angry to begin with? And even if our anger is completely justified, is it productive? Does it get us what we want, or is it "full of sound and fury, signifying nothing"?

Jesus taught: If you are angry with your brother, do something about it. Go directly to your brother with your grievance and talk it out. Don't gossip. Don't hold it all inside. Don't kick the family dog—or your spouse and children. Take your aggravation to the source. For when you confront the other person, you have entered into dialogue and created an opportunity for the Spirit of God to lure you into partnership. For while we may address God in the solitude of our devotional life, it is in the confrontation of human being with human being that God addresses us.

When confrontation doesn't work, try mediation. Jesus prescribes seeking the help of two or three members of the church. If that fails, he instructs, try laying your grievance before the church governing council or the entire congregation (Matt. 18:15-17). The Apostle Paul gives similar advice, chastising the Corinthians for taking their squabbles into the secular courts and urging them to appoint a member of the church as a mediator when disputes arise (I Cor. 6:1-8). *These directives on mediation are probably the most neglected verses in the Bible!*

Jesus regards the presence of unreconciled disputants within a community as destructive to the spiritual and social well-being not only of the foes but of the community as well. Making peace with one's fellow Christian is considered more important than fulfilling one's religious obligations. Insulting a brother or harboring resentment toward him is a violation of the spirit of the Commandment: "Thou shalt not kill." Jesus realized that unvented anger is more explosive than dynamite, and just as lethal.

The remedy that Jesus recommends is forgiveness. To paraphrase his teaching: Get your head out of the past with its hurts and resentments. Put yourself into living relationship—here and now. Don't get even; get together. To withhold forgiveness is to condemn oneself to life's rubbish heap. Each party of a dispute is right and each is wrong. And no matter what the other person did or said, rage wells up from personal reservoirs of spite that existed long before the argument at hand.

We are really angry because we have not been loved

as we perceive we ought to have been loved. Is this perception true? It is and it isn't. We are all the victims of the victims of the victims. At birth, we were placed in the hands of imperfect human beings. No matter how conscientious they may have been, they could never give us the sense of self-acceptance for which we yearned because no one ever gave it to them. On the other hand, our demands for acceptance and approval are boundless. For the first few years of our lives, each of us believes that he or she is the center of the universe, that his or her will is all-powerful, and that just wishing for comfort, affection, and pleasure can bring immediate gratification. When we are thwarted by reality, we pout, wail, and throw tantrums. Not getting our way is the first cause of anger. Not being loved enough is our first excuse.

Our own basic anger causes us to exaggerate what has happened, to see the other person through a filter of self-justification and prejudice and to color our recollections to suit our needs. To emphasize the point that holding on to our grievances lessens our humanity, Jesus adopts the radical stance that our forgiveness by God depends on our willingness to forgive others. (The apostles appealed instead to the example of God: As we have been forgiven, so ought we to forgive others.)

Being able to forgive is a matter of gaining perspective—of realizing that anger invents or exacerbates its own causes. Forgiving is a matter of accepting oneself as flawed and imperfect and as the cause of one's own deepest hurts and disappointments. Forgiveness for others begins with an internalized awareness that God in Christ has reconciled us to himself, that he loves us despite our unworthiness. God's acceptance of us bestows worth and lovability on us. When we accept God's forgiveness, we forgive ourselves; and when we accept ourselves, it is a small task to impute acceptability to others.

Forgiveness also grows out of appreciation and thankfulness, out of the perception that those who love us today and those who have loved us since birth are gifts of God. The grateful heart returns generosity for generosity, kindness for kindness, and in the process of loving, forgiveness is spontaneous. If someone who owes me a hundred dollars gives me a gift of a thousand, will I harbor a grudge about the debt to me?

Forgiveness does not remove responsibility. The forgiven person is still responsible for his actions, still accountable. When I forgive a friend, I ignore the friend's excuses. I do exactly what God has done in Christ, I accept my friend's guilty plea and release him or her with time served, accepting him or her in God's general amnesty. I hold my friend accountable only for his or her words and deeds—not for my projections upon the words and deeds. To forgive is to avoid exaggerating or plugging today's annoyances into yesterday's store of grievances. Forgiveness means recognizing the reservoir of resentment within oneself and knowing that what our friend has done has nothing to do with it. And, finally, I realize that when I confront the obdurate, insensitive resistance in others (or in myself), I do not have to act as an instrument of retribution. There is a cosmic justice that sees to it that in the case of deliberate, harmful behavior the punishment always fits the crime. That punishment is that we are who we are, and we cannot escape from ourselves.

Christian counselors should not attempt to deprive their friends of their right to be angry. Rather they should concentrate on helping a friend understand his or her boiling point, habitual responses, and the consequences of those responses. Further, they should encourage the resolution of conflicts between the friend and others. Conflict is unavoidable. It is also a creative opportunity. Suggestions for responding to the needs of an angry friend are as follows:

1. *Don't cut off your friend's anger.* Let this person express it fully within the safe context of your friendship. Listen. Draw her or him out. Help your friend analyze what is really happening and his or her role in it. And listen again.

2. *Look for the pattern of behavior through which your friend expresses annoyance.* Help your friend become aware of his or her automatic responses to annoyances.

3. *Determine whether the response is creative or destructive.* It is not true that anger never accomplishes anything. Encourage your friend to ask: "Is my anger a reasonable response to an unreasonable situation or an unreasonable response to a reasonable situation? Is it productive? Does it help me get what I want or does it make a fool out of me?"

4. *Suggest forms of expression that enable your friend to accomplish what he or she wants to accomplish.* You may want to point out that anger can never really be talked out, and that getting into the habit of bringing one's anger to a third party may actually make that person more angry. Rehearsing one's anger with a concerned listener is not necessarily cathartic. What is required to release anger is (a) a plan of action (e.g., mediation) for dealing with the direct cause of the anger, (b) an understanding that most anger has nothing to do with what occasions it, or (c) deliberate refocusing of one's energies on anything but the cause of the anger.

5. *If your friend is angry with a third party, design a forum for conflict resolution.* If you are acquainted with both parties, arrange for both of them to have lunch with you and another mutual friend. Clear the plans in advance so neither party will be surprised. If they are both

members of your church, ask your minister and church elders to intervene. If they are members of different congregations, suggest that a committee comprised of members of both churches arbitrate and dispute. Through the reference department of your public library or the information and referral staff in your county department of social services, discover existing resources for keeping disputes out of the courtroom and resolving them on a neighbor-with-neighbor basis. Also many communities have Christian legal aid societies, which offer mediation services based on biblical precepts.

6. *If your friend is angry with you, don't be defensive, be creative.* You probably don't deserve your friend's anger. So what? Your friend's anger probably has nothing to do with you anyway. Listen carefully to the complaints. Help this friend articulate his or her resentment. Agree. You probably are insensitive, inconsiderate, and vexing—at times. (Perhaps not at the particular times the friend is complaining about.) Apologize even if you are in the right—this time. It won't hurt you to see the situation from his or her point of view. (Do this up to the biblical 490 times. Then you are entitled to stand your ground, display righteous indignation, and assert your grievance!)

7. *If you are angry with your friend, forgive.* Cool down. Sort out whether *your* anger is a reasonable response to an unreasonable situation or an unreasonable response to a reasonable situation? It has become popular to say, "I don't get angry; I get even." Think instead: "I do get angry; I get reconciled."

THE REWARDS AND PENALTIES OF BEING A PEACEMAKER

Jesus declared: *"Blessed are the peacemakers."* Peacemakers are loved and esteemed by God but, as a human being among human beings, they must be prepared to sacrifice self-esteem, pride, the assurance that they are right and their brother or sister is wrong (even when they are right and the brother or sister *is* wrong), and much more. For peacemaking has its rewards and its penalties. On the plus side:

You will be respected. Some of your friends will appreciate your counsel and will let you know that you have made a difference in their lives. They will tell you that you are warm, sensitive, caring, compassionate, and empathetic. They will say that you remind them of Moses, Jesus, St. Francis, Kahil Gibran, Gandhi, or Leo Buscaglia.

Occasionally two or more of your friends will even tell one another how much they value you. Somehow their high opinion of your judgment will find its way to you. You will find out that they are saying such things as, "I've spent ten thousand dollars on psychotherapists, social workers, lawyers, and psychics, and none of them helped me as much as our friend did in a ten-minute conversation we had while we were in line together at the check-out stand."

You will gain self-esteem. The appreciation shown by your friends will make you feel good about yourself. When you hear from people you hardly know that you are respected by the friends who have taken your advice, you will realize that you are a person of exceptional worth. You may even feel like sitting on a park bench and waiting for the world to come to you so you can tell it how to straighten itself out. You will indubitably sense that in the time it takes for you to whittel away a stick or knit a few stitches, the leaders of human affairs will surely beat a path to your door. On the negative side:

You will be called a busybody. Your friends and neighbors will tell you to mind your own business. They will accuse you of being a meddler, a fool with nothing better to do than to intrude where you are neither needed nor wanted. You will be called arrogant, boring, silly, stupid, insensitive, and ill-mannered.

You will be misunderstood by those who turn to you for help. Your motives will be questioned. Your friends will demand to know what you really want, what's in it for you. They will accuse you of having caused their problems in the first place, of trying to make them unhappy, of acting high and mighty, morally superior, and spiritually arrogant. You will hear a lot of Bible verses such a "Physician heal thyself" and "Remove first the beam which is in your own eye."

You best advice will be ignored. Just when the solution to your best friend's dilemma of twenty years becomes clear to you, you will discover to your chagrin that your friend would rather find greater disasters on his or her own than accept anybody's advice.

Your worst advice will be followed with tragic results. While you are trying to phone Joan to tell her that you have changed your mind about your advice that she quit her job and start a rural commune, you will get repeated busy signals because she is negotiating the sale of her house with a real estate agent, asking her lawyer to file for divorce, and ordering gardening implements. Joan will lose her husband, children, job, pension, health, and sanity—and blame it all on you.

You tell your mother-in-law that the odds against her winning the state lottery are less than Danny DeVito's at becoming starting center for the New York Knicks. She saves the dollar she had intended to play on the numbers on her poodle's dog license and the next day those numbers are the big winners in the state lottery.

Those whom you advise will do just the opposite of what you recommend and everything will work out fine anyway. You will read the first draft of a novel by your hair dresser's daughter and advise her to go to trade school. Later you discover that she was so insulted that she sent the manuscript to a New York publisher just to show you, and that the rights to the television mini-series alone run to two million dollars. Your daughter will marry that punk rocker that you could never stand, and their marriage will outlast yours.

Your advice is followed, proves sound, but—. Your recommendations are taken with the best possible results. It appears that because of you, your once miserable friends live happily ever after. As the years pass, you become aware that your friends resent you, blame you for totally unrelated problems, and tell lies about you to others.

In sum, there is no reward in mediating, peacemaking, giving advice, or counseling. At least, not in this world. So until you obtain the necessary change of venue, don't expect rewards. Christians counsel because they are who they are. A rose gets no honorarium for its perfume. Some people appreciate its fragrance and others aren't even aware that it exists. The flower has no choice. It can't decide to be anything but a flower. The child of God has no choice but to serve.

PART III

THE COUNSELOR'S CHALLENGE

And do not bring us into temptaion, But rescue us from evil   (Matt. 6:13 LDS).

Then Jesus was led up by the Spirit into the wilderness to be tempted by the devil. And he fasted forty days and forty nights, and afterward he was hungry. And the tempter came and said to him, "If you are the Son of God, command these stones to become loaves of bread." But he answered, "It is written, 'Man shall not live by bread alone, but by every word that proceeds from the mouth of God.' " Then the devil took him to the holy city, and set him on the pinnacle of the temple, and said to him, "If you are the Son of God, throw yourself down; for it is written, 'He will give his angels charge of you,' and 'On their hands will bear you up, lest you strike your foot against a stone.' " Jesus said to him, "Again it is written, 'You shall not tempt the Lord your God.' " Again, the devil took him to a very high mountain, and showed him all the kingdoms of the world and the glory of them; and he said to him, "All these I will give you, if you will fall down and worship me." Then Jesus said to him, "Begone, Satan! for it is written, 'You shall worship the Lord your God and him only shall you serve.' " Then the devil left him, and behold, angels came and ministered to him (Matt. 4:1-11).

And immediately he made the disciples embark into the ship and to go before him to the other side, while he dismissed the crowds. And having dismissed the crowds he went into the mountain to pray alone. And when evening came, he was still there. But the ship was now many furlongs away from the land, being tossed by the waves, for the wind was contrary. Now in the fourth watch of the night, he came toward them walking on the sea. And the disciples seeing him walking on the sea were disturbed saying, "It is a ghost!" and from fear they cried out. But immediately Jesus spoke to them saying: "Have courage, it is I; stop being afraid." And answering him, Peter said, "Lord, if it is you, command me to come to you on the waters." And he said, "Come." And going down from the ship Peter walked on the waters and came toward Jesus. But seeing the wind, he was afraid, and beginning to sink, he cried out saying: "Lord, save me." And immediately Jesus stretching out his hand took hold of him, and said to him: "Little-faith, why did you doubt?" And as they went up into the ship, the wind ceased. And those in the ship worshiped him saying: "The Son of God— that's who you are" (Matt. 14:22-33 LDS).

CHAPTER 10

The Testing of the Christ

Until he was thirty, Jesus lived an ordinary, unremarkable existence as a carpenter, the son of a carpenter, in a provincial backwater. His neighbors apparently knew nothing of the signs and wonders that had attended his birth. They had not been told of the angel's startling conversations with Mary and Joseph, of the manger at Bethlehem, of the shepherds and the heavenly chorus, or of the stargazers who came in search of the newborn king of the Jews. Since the death of the tyrant Herod, the family of Mary and Joseph had lived quietly among the residents of Nazareth. If the Nazarenes were aware of Jesus at all, they knew him for the furniture, tools, and farm implements that he made and repaired. If they honored him at all, it was for the houses and barns that he constructed and embellished.

And then one day he was gone. His neighbors probably thought that he had become bored with small town existence and was headed for the big city, Jerusalem. A few of them might have imagined the truth, that he had gone to see his strange cousin, John the Baptizer. The Nazarenes had heard of John, a notorious "religious fanatic," who haunted the wilderness, preaching to crowds from Jerusalem who sought him out. John said that men should turn away from their unrighteous deeds before the anointed one, the Messiah or Christ, appeared on the scene astride a white horse, sword in hand, to mete out the judgment of God.

For forty days and nights after receiving John's rite of cleansing, Jesus hid in the lonely, empty solitude of the desert and struggled to sort out who he was, to whom he belonged, to whom he was responsible, and to what ministry he had been called. Ignoring thirst and hunger, the scorching heat of the day, the bone-chilling cold of the night, the wind storms and apparitions, he attended only to those terrible conflicting inner voices that contended for possession of his soul. He agonized over what lay ahead as intensely and fervently as his forefather Jacob had wrestled with the angel of God.

During those forty days in the wilderness, Jesus must have thought much about the forty-year odyssey of his ancestors in the desert of Sinai. He recalled how God had sent Moses the deliverer, how he brought the fugitive slaves out of Egypt through the miracle of the Red Sea, how he gave them the Law and bound them to him as his people and himself to them as their God. Jesus remembered the frailty of those freed slaves—their anxieties, their impatience, their lack of faith, and their constant rebellion against their calling and destiny as the chosen people of God. When his own emotions—excitement, loneliness, and confusion—engulfed him, and the desert-born hallucinations became more real than the weariness of his emaciated and dehydrated body, Jesus anchored his being and sanity in the Word of God. He must have recited to himself every syllable of Scripture he could remember. His mind fastened on the book we know as Deuteronomy, the final sermon of Moses to the wilderness nation. Perhaps Jesus started with the Shema, the words most precious to a devout Jew: *"Shema Yisrael, Adonai Elohainu, Adonai Echod"* ("Hear, O Israel, The Lord our God is one Lord," Deut. 6:4.) And then he would have recited the words that follow the Shema: "And you shall love the Lord your God with all your heart, and with all your soul, and with all your might." And a few verses later: "You shall not put the Lord your God to the test" (6:16). A few minutes later, his memory would bring him to the words: "And he humbled you and let you hunger and fed you with manna . . .; that he might make you know that man does not live by bread alone, but that man lives by everything that proceeds out of the mouth of the Lord" (8:3-4). As Jesus started out into the desert, it would have been so appropriate for him to think of Moses and the children of Israel and to recall the final words of Moses contained in the fifth scroll of the Law.

As the words of the Law, Writings, and Prophets ran through his mind, he realized, with an assurance that could never be shaken, who he was, to whom he belonged, and to what he had been called. Then the tempter came!

THE TEMPTATION TO PUT FIRST THINGS SECOND

And the tempter said to him, "If you are the Son of God, command these stones to become loaves of bread." Jesus knew that he was the Son of God. He did not need to prove it to himself. He was also hungry. But he realized that his powers—like those of Moses before him—were not cheap tricks to satisfy his physical needs or his ego. Yielding to just such a temptation had cost Moses entrance into the Promised Land.

Jesus was being tempted to put himself and his needs first and his calling second. He dismissed this temptation with a reference to the heavenly manna that had

fed the Israelites in the desert. What he was saying to
the tempter was, "I will put God first, responding with
the fullness of my being to whom I am, to whom I am
responsible, to my calling. That is all that I can do."

This awareness would echo throughout his ministry.
When those who followed him were more concerned
with food, shelter, and clothing than about the kingdom
of God, the teaching of Jesus was clear: Don't worry
about such things. Seek first God's kingdom and
righteousness and let God take care of the rest (Matt.
6:33; Luke 12:31).

Our first concern should be the God who calls us to
partnership in the ongoing redemptive struggle. "Man
shall not live by bread alone, but by every word that
proceeds from the mouth of God." Where may we
today hear the word that proceeds from the mouth of
God to our ears? It is to be found in the Bible. For the
spiritual message of the prophets, chroniclers, psalm-
ists, sages, evangelists, and apostles will speak to our
hearts if we immerse ourselves in it so that it may wash
over our consciousness, infuse our dreams and aspirations, inform and ennoble our character.

As Protestants, we boast that we are people of the
open Bible. Yet for many of us it remains a closed and
dusty tome. It should be read, studied, meditated upon,
recited aloud, discussed, and cherished. It should not
be worshiped, twisted, distorted, or set above the God to
whom it points, but it surely should never be ignored.

On a more personal level, each of us should listen as
God speaks to us as we fully and without reservation
respond to one another as brothers and sisters in Christ.
For in our age, God does not demand our attention with
unavoidable signs and wonders but whispers to us with
a still, small voice that says, "As you did it to one of the
least of these my brethren, you did it to me" (Matt.
25:40).

Jesus speaks to you and me as individuals—calling each of us to be what he or she alone can be, to use talents and abilities to serve others, to use genius and artistic creativity "to tame the savage beast and make noble the way of man," to meet without whimpering or complaining the challenges, threats, and opportunities of ordinary existence. For to each of us is given a unique direction, a calling, a vocation, a life that may be lived with the fullness and totality of our being.

THE TEMPTATION TO IGNORE REALITY

Next the devil transported Jesus to Jerusalem and placed him on the pinnacle of the Temple, and taunted him: "If you are the Son of God, throw yourself down; for it is written, 'He will give his angels charge of you,' and 'On their hands they will bear you up, lest you strike your foot against a stone.' "

To paraphrase the devil, "If God loves you, you can't get hurt." And by implication, "If you can get hurt, God doesn't love you." It makes sense, doesn't it? And Satan can even quote scriptural justification, the ninety-first Psalm. What is interesting is the way Satan sets the truth of "first things first" on its head. "Seek righteousness first and God will take care of the rest" is twisted into "if you believe in God, you no longer have to take any responsibility for your own life."

Once again, Jesus focuses his attention on the wandering Israelites. No matter what God did for them, they grumbled and complained—just as we do! Instead of receiving the gifts of God with thankfulness and gratitude, they wanted more and more. They were spoiled children demanding, "If you really love me, you will give me what I want." They had lost touch with reality.

Jesus did not succumb to that temptation. He knew how the world was—even for the Son of God. Later, he would teach his disciples to pray: "Lead us not into temptation but deliver us from evil." The Greek text of these words is ambiguous. The words can be translated: "deliver us from *evil*" or "deliver us from *the evil one*. I have often wondered which Jesus had in mind. Were we to ask the Father to deliver us from our own evil inclinations or from the devil?

The writers of the New Testament spoke of evil as a ubiquitous and persistent aspect of our personalities, our experiences, and the world in which we live. They refer to evil hearts, evil thoughts, evil consciences, evil surmising, evil reports, evil days, evil work, evil workers, evil deeds, evil doers, evil men, and evil spirits. They remind us that we live in "the present evil world," that this age is corrupt, out of balance, and insane. The world in which Jesus found himself—and which you and I know—is characterized by suffering, confusion, illness, death, and despair. *God is not the ruler of the world, this present age.* If he were, there would be no suffering, no disease, no death. Evil is king. Sin reigns in us and in our world. It spreads like some hideous disease which invades a healthy body and cannot be destroyed without killing its host.

Sin is not a minor irritation—an occasional outburst of bad manners or a brief time of turmoil that disrupts the habitual peace. War is the natural state of the human race. Discord, calamity, death are the way things are.

Do you remember the news broadcast that interrupted our family gatherings one Sunday years ago? Or the words spoken by our President to Congress on the following day?

Yesterday, Dec. 7, 1941—a date which will live in infamy— the United States of America was suddenly and deliberately attacked by naval and air forces of the Empire of Japan. . . . With confidence in our armed forces—with the unbounded determination of our people—we will gain the inevitable triumph—so help us God.

In the days that followed we set aside pettiness and bickering, and we united as never before to assure the defeat of our common enemies. Along the way, we endured separation, hardship, and shortages, as well as the postponement of career and family plans. Some of our neighbors and loved ones sacrificed a great deal more. For we were convinced, as President Roosevelt confidently predicted on December 9 in his "fireside chat," "We are going to win the war and we are going to win the peace that follows."

> *We interrupt this regularly scheduled program to bring you a special message from God. At every moment of every day since the birth of his Son, special forces under the command of goodness have invaded the human race and begun the final conquest of evil by good. Though God's beachheads are small in our age, our nation, our community, our homes, and our individual lives, God has assured us of his ultimate victory. And he calls on each of us to sacrifice profit, pleasure, and convenience and to join him in this final struggle.*

"You shall not tempt the Lord you God," Jesus insisted. Tempting the Lord is living as if there is no struggle, as if there is no piper to pay, as if we do not reap what we sow, as if it makes no difference what any one of us does, as if there really is a free lunch. "You shall not tempt the Lord your God" means, "Don't leave it to God to do what you are responsible for doing." Don't be careless and claim that you are trusting God.

Don't neglect your spouse, children, parents, or community and say that God will take care of them. Don't shirk the hard work of building your own character or of providing an example of character-building for your children. Don't excuse your failure to keep your word and to honor your commitments by saying, "It's not my fault. That's just the way things are. It must be the way God intended them."

"You shall not tempt the Lord your God" means accept responsibility for your own life. Keep your word. Stop making excuses and stop accepting them.

THE TEMPTATION OF IMPATIENCE

Finally, the devil displayed for Jesus "all the kingdoms of the world and the glory of them"; and the tempter said to Jesus, "All these I will give you, if you will fall down and worship me."

Obviously, the devil considers the kingdoms of the world his to give. God, it would appear, has given him a temporary sublease. Fundamentally, they belong to God, and someday, according to the divine plan, they will revert to his Son. As John proclaims in the eleventh chapter of Revelation (and as we echo whenever we sing Handel's *Messiah*): "Then the seventh angel blew his trumpet, and there were loud voices in heaven, saying, 'The kingdom of the world has become the kingdom of our Lord and of his Christ, and he shall reign for ever and ever'" (11:15). So if they are going to be his anyway, why shouldn't the Son of God claim them now?

The forty days of meditation on the lessons of Deuteronomy reminded him of the forty years in which the children of Israel had tried the patience of God. Jesus realized that even the most faithful continually tempt God through impatience, lack of faith, attempts to force God's hand, desire to do things our way.

Throughout Jesus' career, his audience "tempted" him. The word "temptation" is used in the Gospels to describe an incredible number of encounters between Jesus and the smart alecks of his time. They tried to belittle him, to make him look foolish, and to make themselves look wise; tried to bait him into losing his temper or saying something that would get him in trouble with the authorities; tried to get him to make some grand gesture, such as leading an armed insurrection or calling down fire from heaven against the Romans. But all of the temptations added up to one and the same thing. Jesus was tempted to twist God's arm, to make things happen now, to do things his way rather than God's, to avoid the long, costly road that led to Calvary. He was tempted to override our wills, to make us be obedient and righteous whether we wanted to be or not, to bring in the kingdom of God without having to put up with our confusion, uncertainty, failures, and ineptitudes.

Instead of forcing God's hand, Jesus surrendered himself to the state and fate of humankind. He experienced every temptation (Heb. 2:18). He served us when we should have been serving him. He was obedient unto death, even the death of the cross (Phil. 2:8).

"You shall worship the Lord your God and him only shall you serve." These words remind us that the fear of the Lord is the beginning of wisdom; that for our individual lives to have meaning, we must discover for ourselves a sense of perspective, a feeling of belonging, an awareness that the universe is tilted to reward justice, good conscience, unselfishness.

Is it true? I don't *know*. I can't *prove* it. But I can choose to live it. I can choose to let God be God. I can remind myself daily not to set preliminary concerns before the ultimate; not to let anything less than God be God. I can demand of myself that what I consider important, vital, and central in my life really is important, vital, and central. I can resist the temptation to have to be liked, loved, and appreciated. I can resist the temptation to always have to be right.

We struggle with evil because we have no choice. We wrestle with our own evil inclinations and with the evil one, Satan, the tempter. We are tempted to cut corners, take shortcuts, do it now, do it our way. God's way may be summarized in one word, "serve." "You will worship the Lord your God and him only shall you *serve*." How may I serve you, O king of kings? Again, the still, small voice replies: "As you did it to one of the least of these my brethren, you did it to me." And as Jesus, the disguised king, prepares to lay down his life, he gives a final example—he washes the feet of his disciples (John 13:3-18). He might as well have counseled a friend who was anxious, depressed, confused, or angry. The message would have been the same. Whenever any one of us helps a friend respond to the challenges, threats, or opportunities of his or her life, we serve the King. "If you know these things," Jesus adds, "blessed are you if you do them" (John 13:17).

Despite temptation, Jesus remained focused on who he was, to whom he was responsible, and to what he had been called. The forty days in the desert provided a foundation for his ministry. And despite the rejection by the masses, the instability of his followers, the hostility of the spiritual and civil leaders of his day, he never forgot who he was. In my mind's eye, I see him in the midst of crisis and turmoil returning again and again to the forty days in the wilderness. I hear him whispering to himself the scriptural lessons that gave him the backbone to resist both temptation and the evil one, the scriptural lessons that are every bit as fresh,

meaningful, and significant to us today as we coura-
geously serve, love, and counsel:

"Man shall not live by bread alone, but by every
word that proceeds from the mouth of God."
"You shall not tempt the Lord your God."
"You shall worship the Lord your God and him
only shall you serve."

C H A P T E R 11

The Counselor's Challenge

OPPORTUNITIES FOR COUNSELING

Counseling is a special kind of relationship which exists within all normal associations. For instance, all grandparents are counselors, but not all grandparenting is counseling. Baking cookies is not counseling. Taking grandchildren to the circus is not counseling. Spending the day caring for them while their parents are out of town is not counseling. But it is such fundamental, ordinary interaction that creates the opportunity for counseling.

HOW TO COUNSEL CHILDREN AND GRANDCHILDREN

There are, of course, special opportunities and limitations for each category. Parents have the greatest lifelong influence on their children. They can do the most good or the greatest harm. If parents create an atmosphere in which their children feel accepted, free to communicate, and respected, their children will be open and receptive to their advice—at least, some of the time. The very closeness of the family both intensifies and limits the effectiveness of parents as counselors. (I have devoted chapter twelve to the problems of parents and children.) What they *do*—the example they set, the self-control they maintain, the honesty of their dealings with their family members and with others—is the most powerful educational force in the world.

What parents *say* is another matter. Although children are influenced by their parents' words as long as the parents live and long thereafter, the influence can be positive, negative, or mixed. Ambivalent persons appreciate advice even when they outwardly resist it. There is the natural defensiveness of children when it comes to parental urgings. As children struggle to individuate and achieve independence, they may be poor receivers for parental advice. This does not mean that parents should ignore the problems of their offspring. It simply means that they will have to learn when to offer help and when to back off and allow their children to make their own mistakes.

Most parents are amateurs. Except for the rare parents, who have reared one set of children before starting all over again in their later years, none of us has ever before had the experience of bringing children from infancy to adulthood. There is no training, no instruction manual, and no money-back warranty. Few of us have matured enough to share our time and energy with our children or to allow them to take from us the time and attention of our spouses. Few of us are prepared for the shock of discovering the cost of baby shoes, diapers, toys, a day at Disneyland, a weekend ski trip with the Luther League, or college tuition. For parents, there are never adequate resources—emotionally or financially.

So God created grandparents! Grandma and Grandpa are not beginners. They have had decades to get their act together. They know who they are. They have ironed the bugs out of their own relationship—or, at least, they can cope with each other. They know how to live within their income, and when it comes to children, they have the advantage of experience. They have learned from their mistakes—you!

Parental love is full of *shoulds* and *oughts* and *how many times do I have to tell yous?* Grandparental love is more unconditional—"I love you just because you are." Grandparents can afford to say, "I am always glad to see you," because they always are, and because they know that the grandkiddies will be going home to Mom and Dad at the end of the weekend. I know many people whose inner strength, resilience, and character were achieved despite horrendous parenting. When I ask them how they got to be the persons they are today, they invariably attribute their well-being to the kindness, caring, and unconditional love of at least one grandparent.

The opportunities that grandparents have for influencing their grandchildren are boundless. Grandchildren are often more receptive to the advice of their grandparents than to that of their parents. But as with all close relationships, indirect means are more effective than direct. The small gift, the words of praise, the few extra minutes of attention are the stock and trade of effective grandparental counseling.

Case Notes: Irv

As Irv, a longtime friend of mine, relates:

My grandparents affected me by making me feel of personal worth, by telling me from their longer perspective what the way of the world was, by enabling me to see that my parents were human beings who had passed through the same awkwardnesses I faced and were pretty good role models after all. They had the sense of humor that comes of having seen it all many times. They were able to give without feeling that the gift diminished them or that the recipient owed them anything. (My parents were always concerned about "those nickels and dimes that add up before you know it into the dollars that we need to pay the bills and to save for the new house.") I guess you could say my grandparents were indulgent. They never said no if I asked for a candy bar or an ice cream cone. (My folks would tell me that the sugar would cause cavities or acne.) And I'm not really talking about the few extra dollars they spent on me. It was their spirit. They were generous. They gave of themselves. And they were always so proud of what I did. I just naturally wanted to be like them.

It's not that my folks weren't proud of me. I remember when I got my M.D. They were at the graduation—as delighted as could be. But immediately my dad began asking me why I had accepted an internship at the state hospital instead of Johns Hopkins or Harvard?

My grandfather died when I was still in med school, and my grandmother just after I set up my practice. I don't think that either of them really understood what I was doing. What would a pair of illiterate immigrants from eastern Europe know about dermatology? But they were always happy that I was happy. And their pride—that unconditional love for me just because I was their grandson—shone through in every conversation we ever had.

I asked my friend if his grandparents ever gave him advice. Indeed they had. He told me about one occasion:

I remember taking my fiancee to meet them. At the time, I was having a terrible struggle with my parents. They didn't approve of Theresa because she was of a different religion. My grandparents took to her right off. They urged me to follow my heart.

I think it was always like that. My parents would be concerned about practical consequences. What will the neighbors think? How will your decision affect your ability to make a living? Grandma and Grandpa were more concerned with my happiness. That is not to say that their recommendations were any better; they just came from a different place.

Irv's marriage lasted twenty years, produced three reasonably well-adjusted children, and ended in divorce.

HOW TO COUNSEL YOUR SPOUSE

There are intense marriages that are good marriages. There are intense marriages that are bad marriages. There are dull marriages that are good marriages. There are dull marriages that are bad marriages. No one knows one's foibles and weaknesses better than one's spouse. No one is less capable of doing anything about them. Why? First, there is the issue of "whose problem is this?" It is hard to distance oneself from the situation and to view it objectively. If you need proof, write down all the statements you make to your spouse that begin, "You make me so (happy, angry, sad)." Or "You hurt my feelings when you (said such and such, did so and so, didn't do so and so)." As calmly and as dispassionately as possible, ask yourself how true these statements are. Second, there is the issue of contributory negligence. Perhaps your spouse could stand few alterations, but he or she didn't get to be this way all alone. In some way, you are probably getting exactly what you want (or wanted). Third, as with all counseling, once you open your mouth, you have to accept responsibility for what happens. If you offend a friend, your friend can go home and stew. If you insult your spouse, the house your counselee stews in will be your own.

In situations where you are the one calling attention to the problem, follow these guidelines:

1. *When describing a spouse's problem, avoid making general "you-statements"—especially those containing the words, "always" and "never."* (For example: "You always leave your socks on the bedroom floor" and "You never ask me what I want.") If you are the one who is broaching the issue, use instance-specific, first-person statements: "Let me tell you how I felt when you left the cap off the toothpaste this morning." Note the difference between the following two ways of expressing disappointment when your spouse arrives home forty-five minutes after dinner has been served: (a) "You make me so angry when you're late for dinner; you never appreciate what I do for you," and (b) "I'm angry because you're late for dinner. I'm disappointed that you, the children, and I couldn't eat together."

2. *Convert the blame.* Change "the trouble with you is . . ." into "I know it's probably silly, but when you do such and such, I feel bad."

3. *Accept responsibility for your own feelings.* Try saying: "I felt hurt when you said that (or did that)" instead of "You hurt my feelings when you said that (or did that)." This does not mean that the other party has been given carte blanche to continue behaving in a manner that creates the conditions under which you feel hurt. If the other person is acting responsibly, he or she will get the message.

4. *Never assume that the other person accepts responsibility for his or her feelings.* Never, never say to another person: "I'm sorry you permitted yourself to be hurt" or "It's not my fault that you keep hurting your own feelings

whenever I say that (or do that)." The attitude conveyed would be callous, condescending, patronizing, and dangerous to yourself.

5. *Act responsibly.* Keep your word and make no excuses. Treat the other party as an equally responsible free agent. Expect your spouse to act responsibly, to keep his or her word. Don't ask for excuses.

6. *Negotiate mutual solutions.* Don't assume that your spouse knows what you want or that you know what your spouse wants. Failure to communicate has destroyed more marriages than adultery. Get everything out in the open, seeking third-party help if needed, and then ask, "What can *we* do about this?" Not: "What are *you* going to do?"

HOW TO COUNSEL A FRIEND

A good friend often has both the objectivity and the involvement necessary to serve as an effective counselor. The major problem that friends have is that they would rather offer sympathy and understanding than be agents of change. They assume that this is the wisest course, and it is definitely the most comfortable. But a friend who needs advice or encouragement to transform his or her situation or himself or herself is not well served by passive acceptance. More than once friends who have emerged from a personal or family crisis have asked me why I remained silent when my counsel could have been of "such value." (Just as often, friends have said "thanks but no thanks" when I offered to help, for example, to mediate when they were having problems with a difficult teenager.)

The general guidelines that I have already elaborated

for giving advice and becoming an agent of transformation were written with friends as their object, so I will not repeat them here. But I do want to emphasize the importance of establishing a relationship of mutual caring and sharing as a prerequisite to counseling. A year of supportive, empathetic listening is more important than twenty years of advice-giving. (That is why a good friend is often a greater humanizing influence in one's life than the most devoted parent or spouse. A good friend listens. Parents and spouses have a tendency to tell us what they perceive as being best for us.)

HOW TO COUNSEL A NEIGHBOR

Jesus said the last word on the subject of neighbors in the parable of the Good Samaritan. The trick is to walk the fine line between being (a) alert and available and (b) being meddlesome and obtrusive. I live in the suburb of a large metropolitan city, and I can honestly say that while my house is surrounded by many houses, I have few neighbors. Every now and then, an automobile approaches one of the houses, a garage door opens as though by magic, and an automobile disappears into a garage. Perhaps fences make good neighbors, but garage door openers make none. Being neighborly is an art that requires patience, discipline, and creativity. Being accepted as a neighbor depends on circumstances beyond the control of mere mortals. It is easier to find a silver dollar in a sewer than a true neighbor in a suburb!

When it comes to the people who make their rare appearances outside their garages, those occupants of the houses adjacent to and across from yours, don't confuse them with neighbors until you are able to perform some neighborly act on their behalf and they on yours. Be helpful, hospitable, and cordial, but offer your services as a counselor with extreme caution. You never know as much about them as you think you do, and you may be in a poor position to follow up. So ply your calling carefully.

HOW TO COUNSEL A STRANGER

I call this "Strangers on the Train" counseling. You find yourself next to a total stranger while you are traveling, or waiting in line, or eating at a lunch counter. You or the stranger strike up a conversation. The stranger begins telling you his or her deepest and darkest secrets. Because it is unlikely that the information will find its way back to family, friends, or employer, the stranger talks about problems, infidelities, alcoholism, theft of company funds, or cheating on his or her income tax. Usually hearing this confession in a public place is the only contact that you will ever have with this person or the only person or the only service that you will provide. Sometimes these strangers will ask you to help them, to give them advice, to involve yourself on their behalf, to smuggle their wife or husband into the country, to provide them with food and shelter, to pick up illegal drug for them, whatever.

It is difficult to establish guidelines for chance encounters. There is definite risk as well as opportunity. I suppose that the mugged stranger in the parable could have turned on his benefactor and robbed him, or later sued him for practicing medicine without a license. I am also aware that *every one who is now significant to me was at one time a stranger*. Because the stranger and I were each open to being befriended and to being a friend, a relationship was born. So within the limits of good sense, be open and neighborly, be willing to listen, and, in accordance with the normal guidelines for advice-giving, express your opinions if you are asked for them, but don't attempt to expect too much.

CHAPTER 12

Family Counseling

JOURNEYS TO JERUSALEM

The transition from Christmas to New Year's Day always seems a kind of emotional no-man's land to me. Christmas with all its warm togetherness and sentiments of peace is behind us and the fun and frolic of the arrival of the next year is a week away. We try not too successfully to settle into our everyday routines, all the while knowing that we are performing a charade of respectability and responsibility that fools no one. I note a similarly strange transition in the second chapter of the Gospel According to Luke. At one instant, we are in Bethlehem with Mary, her infant son, and shepherds as angels proclaim, "Glory to God in highest, and on earth peace, good will to men." A verse later, we are in the Temple at Jerusalem for the ritual of circumcision, as the eight-day-old baby Yeshua or Joshua or, as we know him, Jesus is dedicated by his family through an ancient ritual to belong to the convenant that God had made with the descendants of Abraham, Isaac, and Jacob, the covenant later crystallized for all time in the Law of Moses.

A few verses later, with no mention by Luke of the sojourn in Egypt, we are again in Jerusalem for the

Feast of Passover, the great reminder to the covenant people of the God who had chosen them and led them out of Egypt with a strong hand. Now Jesus is a young man, an adolescent discoursing with experts about the law. He is a pre-teenager who had not bothered to tell his parents of his whereabouts, who in the first assertion of his role as giver of the new covenant begins to go his separate way, to pursue his heavenly Father's business, to be in his Father's house, and to cause his parents the pain and anxiety of leaving them in order to do what he had been born to do.

As we know, there would be yet another journey to Jerusalem. This final journey, also recorded by Luke, began with joyful praises, "Blessed is the King who is coming in the name of the Lord!" An irate Jesus drove out the peddlers and provoked his own death at the hands of the guardians of the establishment.

Three journeys to Jerusalem. The first for circumcision, to tell the world that this child belongs to his people and their ways. The second for Passover, the account of which declares that this child is almost an adult, responsible for his own actions, ready to take his place freely as one of us and yet ready to be what only he can be. The third visit begins with the triumphant entry. Jesus condemns us for our failings, questions the very foundation of our institutions. We kill him. Yet instead of destroying the threat, we enable him to accomplish his mission, to fulfill one contract or covenant, and through his death and resurrection to establish for all nations and peoples the very meaning of his name, "God is salvation!"

In our own way, each of us who is called to counsel must make these journeys to Jerusalem. And so too must all we counsel—our friends, neighbors, and loved ones. We are each a child of the covenant. We are bound by the fact of birth to our mother and father, to siblings, aunts, uncles, grandparents, and cousins. We are the potential fulfillment of their individual and collective hopes. We are shaped and fashioned by their every glance, word, and deed. As long as we live, we are theirs. We belong to them. We will struggle with this identity, with their expectations, and with their values long after they have passed from this earthly stage.

Some of us are products of relatives who loved us, comforted us, were there for us, and, since they were only fallible human beings, failed, and even neglected us now and then. We must nurture that child, live every day with thanks for those who cared and learn through their failures unless we want to repeat them in our own parenting. To some of us as children, much was given and of us little was expected. And in so many ways, nothing has changed. God gives freely and we are loved, when we but let ourselves be loved.

The family is the system in which each of us lives, and moves, and has his or her being. As a counselor, strive in every way to build and reestablish the supportive family structure of those whom you counsel. No matter how badly damaged a marriage may be, no matter how strained the fabric of the family may have become through distance and circumstances, invest your efforts, first and foremost, in rebuilding the family. And if such efforts are impossible, help establish a new family of loving, supportive brothers and sisters. Thre are many ways of adopting "orphans of fate." Invite those separated from their families by distance or divorce to spend Thanksgiving, Christmas, and occasional week-ends with your family. Encourage your church to plan special social events as though it were a large, extended family. Blessed is the person who finds in the fellowship of the faithful many mothers and fathers, brothers and sisters, and blessed in the eyes of God is anyone who accepts another into his or her family.

As much as the support of others enhances our becoming all that we are capable of being, each of us remains fully responsible. Each of us must listen to the voice of God, and when each of us responds to the calling of God, to the unique vocation that sets us apart, we must risk losing the secure identity as someone's child or disciple or pupil or employee or spouse. Each one must take the chance of being misunderstood by peers and loved ones. It is not easy to be about our Father's business nor is it easy to let go of our children so that they may respond to the One who calls them.

The counselor must recognize that even the best of families—either biological or spiritual—must ultimately disintegrate in a natural way. The goal of counseling is the final freedom from all that limits the counselee, including his or her relationship with the counselor. The test of a loving family is its ability to respect the decisions made by its members, even if these decisions are painful, confusing, and alien to that family. As both counselor and parent, I must grant those whom I love the same freedom I demand for myself.

None of us is called to make the final trip to Jerusalem. Christian theology tells us that Jesus did that for us one and for all. And yet he walks that road in and through us today. He calls us to die to self and be reborn as instruments of God's peace and justice. Jesus would not accept business as usual. He would not accept the excuses of those who compromised principle because it was convenient and profitable. He warned of the judgment that was about to befall his nation. In forty years, the Temple would be gone, the people dispersed. In forty, fifty, sixty, seventy years, all of us will likewise be gone. And if our lives are to count for anything, we must reexamine and reassert our covenants, our personal trips to Jerusalem. Each of us must ask, To whom do I belong? Whose child am I? Whose love and caring made me the person I am today? What mistakes did they make? How can I learn from those mistakes?

What do I stand for? What do I believe? What kind of world do I want for myself and my children?

What is my calling? What is my mission? Am I willing to nurture a sense of my truest, highest self? Whose business am I about? In whose house do I reside?

Can I serve even if there are no triumphant hosannas and thank-yous? Can I humbly and gratefully accept the love that God showers on me through those who love me for myself when I let them?

And can I as a Christian counselor adopt those who need the family life that I can help provide? In the end, can I honor their freedom and be delighted when they need me no longer?

IDENTIFYING THE REAL "CLIENT"

For several years, as executive director of a family crisis counseling center, I dealt with parents who were distressed by a son or daughter's involvement in one or more of the following forms of behavior:
—conversion to a cult
—a mixed marriage
—drug experimentation
—relocation away from the family home
—homosexuality
—dropping out (e.g., leaving high school or college, or choosing not to take one's place in a family-owned business)
—penury and joblessness
—divorce
—deciding not to have children
—a bizarre, health-threatening diet

—pursuing a strange vocational choice (e.g., leaving law school to become a farmer or giving up a medical practice to become a hang-glide instructor)

—showing preference for one parent over the other after a parental divorce

In many instances, what these parents wanted was a miraculous conversion. They wanted me to talk their son or daughter out of the decisions, behavior, or way of life that their parents found objectionable.

Families have expectations regarding their children—even when those children become adults and have children of their own. These expectations are neither inventions nor the products of spontaneous generation. Conceptions of acceptable behavior, proper conduct, valuable careers, responsibility, and duty are cultivated by a society as though they were crops. Although the process is inefficient (since it is often characterized by waste, error, outmoded assumptions, inconsistency, and inadequate resources), it is supported by all the institutions of society including government, education, and the church. Families and the greater society can be quite coercive in enforcing their demands. When they encounter obstinate resistance, they call on agencies of social control such as the police, social services, mental health professionals, and clergy to support them. In addition, they resort to guilt-tripping, intimidation, bribes, and other maneuvers to achieve their ends.

Seldom does the problem reported by the parents initiate family dysfunctions, although it clearly intensifies them. Often the problem of the moment is an excuse to renew a long-term struggle for power within the family. At times, the desire to punish and the need to control stand out like a midnight bonfire on a hilltop.

When most of the parents came to the counseling center, their assumption was that their offspring had a serious problem, was in big trouble, and needed to be rescued. For purposes of my intervention, they were identifying their son or daughter as my client. My assumption, on the other hand, was that since they were distressed, they were my real clients. Before doing anything I had to answer one fundamental question for myself, Who really needs my help? In other words, whose problem are we really dealing with—that overanxious parents or of a son or daughter who may have gotten in over his or her head?

The counselor must always ask, Whose problem is this? Who is the real object of my caring and intervention? Who really needs me? In my professional counseling of distressed families, my routine is as follows: First, I attempt to assess the family dynamics, accumulated misunderstandings, poor communications, and hostilities that have contributed to the present problem. Then, I involve the family members who have come to me in developing a strategy, assigning roles to the spouses, parents, family members, or friends. Then I delegate to family members or friends the job of establishing contact, developing trust, and creating opportunities for dialogue. Where it is appropriate, I enter this dialogue and provide the client my services as a mediator and a guide. I act as megaphone, making sure that each side hears and comprehends the concerns of the other side. I attempt to sort out the apparent incompatibilities and provide an objective point of view. I offer the identified clients the opportunity to hear my version of the story. I help them gain a perspective from which to judge the issues for themselves.

When I first meet them, most of the identified clients are so immersed in what they are doing that they have no objectivity, no ability to examine critically what they are doing. Further, they are defensive, holding on to the life-style that they have chosen as though their very lives depended on it, resisting their loved ones as if this were the last chance of their lives to assert their freedom from parental control. As I have learned from hundreds of clients, this is not the whole story, for everyday they hear a still, small voice that asks them if they really like the existence they have chosen, if they really want to continue. Many clients do not give me an opportunity to say more than a few words before they interrupt me with the question, "Do you really think I'm doing the right thing with my life? Is there any way that I can change? Can you help me get back together with my mom and dad? I really hate what I'm doing and want to get out." And I give permission to such clients to do exactly what they want to do.

So whenever a personal or a family problem is presented to you, ask yourself first, Whose problem is this? Then, ask again, for the answer may be elusive. The language in which human suffering expresses itself is essentially self-centered, exaggerated, and self-serving. When you have a sure sense of who the object of your efforts really is, assess who can help. In a distressed family, there is usually a sibling or a parent who has close emotional ties with the identified client, and, hence, the greatest leverage or influence.

Develop a team effort to reconcile the family members, planning as carefully as you would a social event for four hundred couples. In a deliberate, step-by-step manner, contemplate who will approach the identified client, what should be said, what objections may be expected, how they may be overcome, what the role of each relative or friend will be, what is expected of the counselor, what outcomes (positive and negative) may be anticipated, how each involved party will follow up, and so forth. And remember that the goal of family counseling is making the family work for each member—not the restoration of the wayward individual to conformity with parental expectations.

Case Notes: *Arnold and Hank*

Arnold is the coach of the Pee Wee League Baseball team. He is thirty-five. The team members are nine. Arnold is aggressive, competitive, and demanding. The kids are clumsy, uncoordinated, and inattentive. Arnold knows baseball inside and out. The kids are not sure if a walk is three balls or four.

Arnold not only coaches the team, his business sponsors it. The back of each uniform reads, "Yankees—Arnold's TV and Stereo." When Stevie Ferguson showed up with a dirty jersey, Arnold benched him. When Bobbie Ramano was tagged out running into third base instead of sliding, Arnold berated the child for five minutes, calling him a "wimp" and a "chicken." When Tony Anderson was called out on a close play, Arnold accused the first base umpire of favoritism, insisted that the ump be replaced and that his call be reversed, and pulled his team off the field until his demands were met.

Hank is also thirty-five. He is teaching soccer to a newly formed boys' team in the recreational department program. I watch him work with his collection of seven- to ten-year-old boys as I walk my dogs. "That's the way, Joey," he cries to the tiniest player. "Joey, Joey, he's our man! I knew you'd make a great goalie." "Way to go, Keith!" he yells as a nine-year-old moves the ball across the playing field. Another player blocks Keith's path and maneuvers the ball away from him. "Yeah, Phil," Hank exclaims. "Looking good, Phil."

After thirty minutes, Hank calls time. "You guys are champs! Tell your parents not to be surprised if there are scouts from professional teams at all our games!" And then he dismisses them.

Both Arnold and Hank are fathers. Arnold has three sons, no daughters. Hank has one son and one daughter. I wonder what it is like to be their children and what the future holds for them. Will Arnold's sons become aggressive, assertive, demanding, and self-centered? Will they share their father's love for baseball? Or will they turn out shy, introspective, and morose with no interest in athletics? And will Hank's children share his zest for life? Will they believe in themselves? Will they want to serve others as enthusiastically as their dad does?

ADVICE TO PARENTS

Frequently parents ask me how they can "cult-proof" or "drug-proof" their sons and daughters. I tell them that the best defense against the problems of the young adult years is to create during childhood days an atmosphere of free and open communication. Most of the young adults I counsel feel that they were never able to discuss their deepest feelings with anyone—family, friends, or professionals. They report a wall of retience, busyness, and impatience that stood between them and their parents during their adolescent and college years. The willingness of the instant family provided by the cult or sect or their drug-using peers to listen sympathetically is for many clients their first experience of unconditional emotional support. Or so it seems.

Protecting a child against tomorrow's follies requires a deepening of interpersonal intimacy, the willingness to listen, and more. While teaching college classes during the sixties and seventies, I was often thanked by my students for encouraging them "to think for themselves." I wondered for whom they had been thinking during the previous twenty years. Being autonomous is an art that requires constant practice and much support. Keeping the next generation of children out of trouble requires that we carefully and cleverly explain to them how everyday decisions are influenced by peers, advertising, parental expectations, and one's own insecurities. We need to praise independence and responsibility in decision making. The real villain is gullibility—the inability to examine our actions critically and the unwillingness to say no.

Cults, drugs, and antisocial life-styles have little fascination or power of attraction for those who know who they are, what they believe, how to think for themselves, and where their lives are going. Parents can do a great deal to encourage the development of a sense of identity, to foster a positive self-image, and to provide an island of unconditional acceptance in the midst of a lonely and threatening world. Parents can and should articulate ethical values and religious beliefs. None of these actions can guarantee that one's offspring will be happy, successful, or trouble-free. Not doing them is a prescription for disaster.

Remember *attitudes are caught not taught.* Children imitate the only role models they have—their parents. Children have no innate knowledge about religion, money, sex, interpersonal relationships, or anything else.

The child of parents with clear commitments has something against which to react, attitudes to reject or refine, and a haven to which he may return if all else fails. "Live and let live" provides no sense of direction. No one can find a fixed point of reference in a stress-filled world by reacting to such an attitude as that reflected in the often-heard parental copout: "I don't believe in forcing my children to do anything they don't want to. I think they should have the right to think for themselves, to decide on their own values and beliefs. I think that when they are adults they can choose their own religion, morality, and politics." If only parents who feel this way would realize that they are telling their children: "I really don't care what you believe or how you choose to behave as long as you don't hurt yourself or embarrass me. I just make out the best I can from day to day. I don't know what I believe; so how can I encourage you to follow in my steps?" How much better it would be if we admitted our own lack of faith to our children instead of patting ourselves on the back for our superiority to those who compel their children to conform to parental standards of faith and practice.

I think a much sounder approach is strengthening self-image, enhancing the ability to communicate feelings and needs, and emphasizing the importance of accepting responsibility for one's own decisions. And I also think that careful consideration of a child's moral and religious education cannot be neglected. From all outward appearances, we are one of the most religious societies in the history of the world. The vast majority of us believe in God, consider ourselves Christians, regard Jesus as divine and the Bible as God-inspired, and belong to a church. But most of us provide our children with less guidance on religious matters than we do on how to mow the lawn.

The fundamental role of the parent as counselor (and as parent) is setting an example. Equally important is reinforcing positive behavior with praise and affection. The family can avail itself of an opportunity that no other institution can equal for instilling values, creating an atmosphere for the safe expression of needs, and molding character. To be successful, parents must observe the same rules as any counselor. (See "Rules for Giving Advice," pages 56-58.)

Even as parents have responsibilities to their children, so too are children responsible toward their parents. In childhood, sons and daughters should honor and obey their parents. A family is not a democracy. It is more like a constitutional monarchy. Someone has to accept the responsibility for providing food, shelter, education, and guidance. With such awesome responsibility should come respect. For a child to withhold respect from a parent is as serious as a parent withholding love and sustenance from a child. As a counselor, I am appalled when I hear a parent demand the respect that he or she thinks is due. More than once, I have heard the words of the Apostle Paul cited: "Children, obey your parents in the Lord, for this is right. 'Honor your father and mother' (this is the first commandment with a promise), 'that it may be well with you and that you may live long on the earth' " (Eph. 6:1-3).

In most of these cases, the child (usually a teenager or adult) could just as equitably demand that the parent live up to the rest of Paul's advice: "Fathers, do not provoke your children to anger, but bring them up in the discipline and instruction of the Lord" (Eph. 6:4).

When I witness such disputes, I am aware that each side is expressing many years' worth of resentment. Each party is really saying to the other, "You do not love me as much as you ought to." The parent is saying, "I have given you all this and you will not even give up thus-and-such for me." The child is saying, "If you really loved me, you would let me live my own life." Unfortunately, such disputes harden into "win or lose" confrontations. One party gets his or her way and the other party gets nothing.

If parents would for just a moment put the role as counselor first, they would be eager to listen, to listen again, to hear their child's implicit complaint, "you don't love me enough to trust me," and would be willing to negotiate a resolution. If children would put their role as counselor first, they would listen until they have heard their parent's implied plea to them, "Love me as much as I have loved you."

Parents counsel by example. Children counsel by following that example and by being appreciative. There is a folk tale about a mother bird who is able to rescue only one of her three fledglings from a rising tide. She asks each of her offspring in turn why she should save him. The first says, "Save me, and I will take care of you in your old age." The second says, "Save me, and I will sing so beautifully that all the creatures of the forest shall be made glad." The third says, "Save me, and I will care for my children as dutifully as you have cared for me." The mother rescues the last one.

Here is a brief exercise, "Crossing the Time Barrier," that may help you respond to the needs of your parents. Begin with the parent with whom you have an ongoing problem, the one whose demands you can never live up to. Calculate the year that he or she was exactly the same age as you are now. In your imagination, recreate that year. Who was president? What were the major news events? Who received the Academy Awards? Who won the World Series, the Stanley Cup, and the Super Bowl (or the NFL championship)? What were the most popular songs, novels, plays, nonfiction books?

Now, think of the major problems, difficulties, and challenges of our present life. Imagine what it must have been like to deal with them a generation ago. Give yourself as strong a sense as possible of the year when your mother or father was your age. Imagine the sights, sounds, sensations, and odors of those days. Examine family photographs, "interview" your parents and relatives about the year in question. Rent a video tape of a movie that depicts the year or one made during that time. When you have a firm fix on the year, think of the time and place in which you find yourself today. What is in the headlines? What songs are being played? How would you describe life today in your family, your community, your nation if you were being interviewed by a journalist from another country, another world, or another time?

For example, my father and mother were born in 1915 and 1916, respectively. At the time of this writing, I am forty-seven. My parents were both my age in 1963. A summary of 1963 can be found in the "U.S.A.—Year by Year, 1770–1975" article in *The People's Almanac*[1] or in *The Encyclopedia of American Facts and Dates*.[2] With help from these sources, I recall the following: John F. Kennedy was president. He was assassinated on November 22, 1963. *Lawrence of Arabia* was the picture of the year. *Who's Afraid of Virginia Woolf?* and *A Funny Thing Happened on the Way to the Forum* won the Tony Awards. On our radios and phonographs, we listened to Tony Bennett singing "I Left My Heart in San Francisco," a Belgian nun's tribute to "Dominique," and the Peter, Paul, and Mary rendition of "If I Had a Hammer." The Los Angeles Dodgers swept the New York Yankees in four games. (Sandy Koufax struck out fifteen players in the opening game.) American involvement in Vietnam steadily increased. "Pop art" was featured at the Guggenheim Museum in New York. Medgar Evers, a Mississippi civil rights leader, was shot to death. Over two hundred thousand blacks and whites marched for civil rights in Washington, D.C., and listened to keynote speaker, Martin Luther King, Jr.,

---

1. David Wallechinsky and Irving Wallace, *The People's Almanac* (Garden City, N.Y.: Doubleday, 1975).
2. Gorton Carruth et al, eds., *The Encyclopedia of American Facts and Dates*, 8th rev. ed. (New York: Harper & Row, 1987).

proclaim, "Now is the time to rise from the dark and desolate valley of segregation to the sunlit path of racial justice."

What must it have been like to be forty-seven then? To face what I am facing now? To know that the number of remaining productive, adult years is less than the number that have already passed? To be more concerned with being a grandparent than a parent? To face the prospect of living without one or both of your own parents? To have aches, pains, and gray hair tell you that you are no longer young? To be as respected and appreciated as you will ever be?

By focusing on that with which I am best acquainted—my problems and concerns of today—and on the specific setting of my parents' world when they were my age, I am able to identify with them, to be as understanding and forgiving of them as I am of myself, to let go of resentment, and to feel again the fundamental oneness of our relationship. To the extent to which I am able to understand and sympathize with my parents when they were my age, I am able to realize much more than that "we are all the victims of the victims of the victims." I am able to realize that, all things considered, they faced their problems and their world just as bravely, creatively, and humanely as I do mine. It is not only from their mistakes that I have learned. Their example, it turns out, has influencd me more than I would ever admit. For it turns out that "we are all the beneficiaries of the beneficiaries of the beneficiaries."

The irony of being a parent and being a child is that with each passing year the roles become more and more reversed. Mom and Dad begin to need advice, nurture, and security. Son and daughter need to be needed. Is there ever a point of balance—a point at which parents and children are peers, equals, and friends while still remaining parents and children? Somewhere in the fifty years or so of relatedness, there may be a few years. No relationship is more fulfilling or magic, but it does not come by accident. Such rapport must be tended, fed, and cherished.

Partnership in Suffering

Case Notes: *Joe*

Joe, a friend of mine, is dying. The therapy that extends his remaining months is painful and exhausting. He is in his forties and has a wife and three children. He is a minister of the gospel. His parishioners, attempting to comfort him, are always telling him to accept his lot as the will of God. He becomes angry and tells them that he cannot worship a God who would allow him to suffer and would leave his family without a husband and father. Joe tells them: "Disease and death are *not* the will of God. They are the consequences of a world out of control, a world that shunned the will of God in the beginning and that continues to shun it at every moment. As it drifts its meaningless way like some great machine run amok, it is killing me, afflicting me with pain, and denying me a future with my loved ones."

Candy

Three years ago, Candy, a fifteen-year-old client of mine, collapsed in a shopping mall in our community. The emergency room staff had to pump her stomach to save her life. She had consumed enough alcohol and tranquilizers to kill herself. She wasn't trying to hurt herself. She just liked the drug-induced high, and kept taking more and more.

Her mother, Sue, has been married and divorced six times. Candy has lived with her mother during the marriages and with relatives during the times between. The girl has not passed an academic course in years and has no other interests except drugs and rock 'n' roll. During our counseling sessions, she is sullen and noncommunicative. She just wants to drift and to be taken care of.

Her mother is dating a millionaire. He has just given her a two-carat diamond engagement ring. I know all about it. Sue talked about little else during our recent one-hour session. We were supposed to be talking about Candy but Sue was too excited to talk about anything but herself. Candy is a cumbersome burden to her. Sue can't understand what's wrong with her daughter. She has everything. Perhaps if we could find the right private school. Money is no object.

(A tragic footnote: I recently learned that Candy has AIDS.)

Wendel

Wendel is the auditor of a chemical company. A year ago he had a vision of Jesus at a pentecostal healing service. At the time, he was about to have surgery for removal of a malignant tumor. During a seven-week period, the tumor spontaneously shrank and disappeared. Wendel began attending pentecostal services seven to ten times a week. He became upset when his wife and children refused to accompany him. He lives alone now. His wife wants him but not his fanaticism. He wants her as well as his newfound faith.

Toni and Ed

Toni is in love with Ed, an alcoholic. At first, he was so grateful for her love that he gave up drinking. They were married and the honeymoon went on for six months. In their presence I felt like a fifth wheel—each was so devoted to the other's every word, sigh, and glance.

Then Ed started drinking again. He seems enraged with Toni half the time and appreciative of her understanding the other half. Her moods match his perfectly. She seems loving and devoted when he is not drinking—at least most of the time. When Ed is the least bit difficult, whether he is drinking or not, she can suddenly become demanding, confrontative, and unreasonable. They trigger the best and the worst in each other. Unfortunately, the worst is becoming more and more frequent.

THE REALITY OF EVIL

Evil is real. Life is unfair. Sometimes nice guys finish last. Hard work is not always rewarded, and we all make mistakes. We all cause harm and grief even when we try to make things better for our friends and loved ones. Among my clients, I note only three categories: those who regret bad decisions, those who put off making decisions, and those who have buyer's remorse about good decisions.

If God is loving and all-powerful, why does he tolerate evil? If suffering is punishment for sin, why is it that the righteous are afflicted while the unrighteous prosper? Why does God let us make mistakes? Why do Christians suffer when they are doing the best they can? Why do so many of our decisions turn out to be disasters? Why do we still feel that we could have done better even after we have made a decision?

The only basis for affirming the meaningfulness of life in the face of the insurmountable evils of human existence is the recognition that the tribulations of humankind are also the sufferings of God, that our struggle to realize good despite all that opposes us is at the same time God's ongoing creation of order out of primal chaos. The process through which peace and harmony are achieved is a divine-human undertaking, a partnership that exposes both humankind and God to opposition, defeat, and pain. Unless God himself participates in the heartache and sorrows of our earthly state, then all striving is in vain.

There is an inner voice that lures each of us toward personal unity and integrity. In this way, the Spirit of God draws us into partnership in the ongoing creative process. For the creation of the universe did not end with the events recounted in Genesis; it only began. Good is that which we do with the wholeness of our being; evil is that which concerns only a part or segment of our total experience. Every time we give ourselves wholly and unconditionally to a single direction, we fail, but such a setback gains for us an inkling of the one true direction. Through risk and failure, we become the unique and whole persons that only we can become. Conscience is the voice that calls the developing self to fulfill the unique and never-to-be-repeated potentialities of its being. Coming to maturity is the coming to be of one's distinctive personality. It is the acceptance of the awesome and terrible responsibility of actualizing one's singularity. Very few individuals are willing or capable of making this dangerous response. There is a trace of cowardice in us all—a willingness to forgo the tensions and sorrows of becoming independent and unique persons.

Evil arises when a person's life remains within itself, centered on security and satisfaction. Self-isolation grows out of the fear of being hurt, the terror of being used, the memory of past mistakes, awkwardness, and humiliation. The self-centered person does not hear the call of God in the interaction with other human beings. Rather the self-centered person drifts without deciding on direction. Evil is the refusal to accept the responsibility for one's own life and the corresponding deafness to the call to respond to any other self.

Good is direction and all that follows from direction. Good is openness to others. Evil is surrender to the momentary and the available, the instantaneous response to whatever presents itself. It scatters the self into a thousand conflicting and contradictory impulses, not two of which can occupy the attention of the individual at the same time. Evil cannot be done with the whole soul. It is a striking out at whatever is at hand. To a person without direction, there is neither right nor wrong. Adam and Eve partook of the forbidden fruit not because they decided to do so but because they were sunk in a trancelike state of contemplation of possibilities that made them oblivious to what they were doing. Cain killed Abel not because he decided to murder but in order to confirm and intensify his basic indecision.

Prolonged indecision constitutes a virtual decision for indecision. Indecision becomes a fixed course of action, a radical dedication to evil. Our movement toward becoming what we can become is arrested by the determination to remain just as we are. When this happens, we become our own creator. We no longer react to others, and because it is in unconditional responding to others that we develop and receive confirmation of who we are, the self-centered individual is cut off from the possibility of growth, change, and self-knowledge. Life becomes a series of carefully executed mimes and poses intended to give the appearance of a developed personality. The hardening process can become irreversible. A point can be reached at which the individual is no longer able to respond to others or to his or her authentic selfhood. The small misunderstandings, failures of judgment, moments of deafness, and unkept promises suddenly harden like cement. The individual has drifted outside the creative stream, away from God's ongoing work of reconciliation.

When we are no longer responsive to the voice of God as he speaks to each of us in our lives as human beings among other human beings, we become totally dependent on some other finite, limited entity to provide us with satisfaction. The inner compass of right and wrong is smashed. The voices of conscience and of community are muffled. We are on our own, and when the issues are too complex for him to make his decisions, we continue to drift, allowing others to think for us, giving them our unconditional dedication in return for their easy answers. God is no longer God. By surrendering our responsibility, we are no longer free. We are enslaved to that which we depend on—a lover, a cause, a sect, a book, an ideal, a drug, a slogan, or a momentary feeling.

Freedom and responsibility are inseparable. Because we are fully free to accept or reject the way set before us by God, we are also fully responsible. Because we are fully responsible, we are fully free. Our rights are our duties. The only right possessed by persons in the political, academic, religious, social, or economic spheres is complete responsibility. Responsibility without freedom is slavery; but freedom without obligation is abandonment to aimlessness, the very essence of evil.

Evil is refusal to enter into relation, the determined puffing up of one's individuality and self-importance so that there is no need for confirmation of one's being by another. Self-made people are capable of dialogue only with their creator—themselves. Their response to other persons is determined by the uses to which they can put them. Authentic love—the acceptance of others as responsibility and a mutual opportunity—is replaced by the distorted affection that regards the other person as a thing to be possessed, as an endless supply of creature comfort, as a boundless private source of personal reassurance. Authentic love asks, How may we help each other grow? How may we affirm each other's potential? Self-centered love considers the other a mirror for the enjoyment of one's own image—an image that is destined never to change.

Sooner or later, self-centered existence destroys the selfish individual and everything he or she loves. The only real atheist is the totally isolated individual. For such persons have cut themselves off from the only place where God can be heard and have denied themselves access not only to God's revelation but to knowledge of who they really are, as well.

Partnership with God is costly. To worship God as God means that one must be open to respond without ever knowing if one is doing the absolutely right thing. To live is to be guilty of inflicting pain and committing injustice. We cannot breathe or eat or walk without destroying life. We make mistakes and will continue to make mistakes. We live in a confusing and evil world—confusing because we project our own confusion on it and evil because it is not yet redeemed, because it is not yet created. The creative spirit that works in each of us enables us to become instruments to peace for ourselves, our neighbors, and for our world. But the process of creation is filled with pain, contradiction, confusion, and suffering. In this suffering we are not alone, for what we experience mirrors the struggle of the divine with us and our world. It is through crucifixion and death that God in Christ reconciles the world to himself. And it is through our courage, our affirmation of life, our turning of chaos into meaning, our suffering and pain, that we are instruments of the divine purpose.

Responding to Depression

Case Notes: Kim

Kim was twenty-five. She was tall, blonde, and solidly built. She had an ingratiating smile, beautiful eyes and features. She also had an abundance of musical talent; she could sing and play the piano as well as any professional. Her parents had encouraged her in every way. She grew up among exciting, talented, and successful people. Her mother was an established portrait painter and her father was the founder of one of the first personal computer companies.

With so much going for her, her life was a study in frustration. In college, she changed her major twice a year, and, after five years, she dropped out, still far from earning a degree. Her love life was disastrous. She tried hard to please the young men in her life, but they all became bored with her and went their separate ways. The only jobs at which she succeeded were menial and exhausting. When I met her, she had been working for three years at minimum wage for a candy company, carrying hundred-pound bags of loose jelly beans and gummy bears from the loading dock and repacking them in one-pound bags.

She wanted to be as successful as her parents and their friends. She was an aspiring rock performer, but she claimed that she was too proud and too talented to have to work her way up the ladder—the dismal round of small clubs, one-night stands, selling herself to a top agent, and knocking on doors of producers. As an acquaintance of hers told me, "The trouble with Kim is that she wants to be on the roof of a ten-story building, but if she can't do in one big leap, she figures, 'I'm a failure. What's the use?' So she spends her time feeling miserable and making everyone who cares about her miserable as well."

Carl

When we first met, Carl was a graduate student at an ivy league university. He was in the ninth year of a ten-year program in philosophy. He had married during his sophomore year of college and managed to support his wife and three children while earning his bachelor's and master's degrees. When I was introduced to him, he was finishing work on his doctoral dissertation. For more than nine years he maintained his sense of balance and good humor despite poverty, a less than ecstatic marriage, and the hazing from faculty and senior students that form the grad student's lot. When we lunched together on campus, I enjoyed his quick sense of humor, his encyclopedic knowledge of an incredible variety of subjects, and his interest in contemporary ethical issues. (We sat on the edge of the reflecting pool together in Washington as we listened to Martin Luther King, Jr., declare, "I have a dream.")

That summer he completed his dissertation and successfully defended it. He accepted a job at a nearby university, had three articles published in scholarly journals, and was offered contracts for books by two respectable publishers. Then, he proceeded to fall apart. He became edgy and irritable. He lost his temper easily and managed to alienate his wife, children, and friends. While we were fishing one day, he told me that he no longer knew what to do with his life, that for ten years he had known exactly what he wanted and had single-mindedly gone after it, but now he felt lost and confused. He asked me if I had ever tried cocaine and began telling me about his recent LSD trips and his extramarital adventures with members of both sexes.

Three years later, he left the university, his wife and

children in order to join a religious commune in Alaska, where he taught kindergarten and repaired farm equipment, but his depression remained as debilitating as ever. He visited me a few weeks ago. He survives on mental disability income from the university, having been unemployed for three years. It is as though the only thing that still remains of the Carl I knew seventeen years ago is his outrageous, self-deprecating sense of humor. He can send me into convulsions of laughter within ten seconds, but the joke is always on him.

Cindy

Cindy, a student in a religion class I taught at Temple University, was extremely shy and obviously discouraged with life. She told me that she considered herself "a very sensitive person." I asked her if by "sensitive," she meant that she was tuned in to the needs of others and responsive to those needs or that her feelings were easily hurt. Without thinking for a second, she blurted, "People are always hurting my feelings, or maybe I'm always allowing myself to be hurt. I guess I'm not sensitive at all. Just overly concerned with my own feelings. What a pain!"

DEPRESSION

Depression is both endemic and epidemic in our society. It spreads its way from mother to child, husband to wife, friend to friend, and finds its way to those who are not in contact with anyone similarly afflicted. Its symptoms, varied but yet related, strike us all. For some of us there is the occasional feeling that life is hopeless and that no one can or will help us. We weather the dark clouds and are pleasantly surprised when the sun returns. A smaller number of us feel discouraged, enfeebled, and powerless most of the time. Not only do our periods of depression differ in frequency, but range in intensity from mild to overwhelming and from bearable to disabling.

To some observers, suspicion, discontent, cynicism, and frustration seem apt descriptions of the general mood of our society. Many contend that ours is an age of scant enthusiasm for the many and of misguided fanaticism for the few. As Kenneth Kenniston states:

The prevailing images of our culture are images of disintegration, decay, and despair; our highest art involves the fragmentation and distortion of traditional realities; our best drama depicts suffering, misunderstanding, and break-down; our worthiest novels are narratives of loneliness, searching, and unfulfillment; even our best music is, by earlier standards, dissonant, discordant, and inhuman. Judged by the values of past generations, our culture seems obsessed with breakdown, splintering, disintegration, and destruction. Ours is an age not of synthesis but of analysis, not of constructive hopes but of awful destructive potentials, not of commitment, but of alienation.[1]

No wonder so many of us seem consigned by some apathetic fate to lives of quiet desperation. Among professional counselors, depression is known as "the common cold of mental illness." Not only does this ailment inconvenience the sufferer, it may also kill him or her. Effective remedies remain elusive. Talking therapy often fails; medication is appropriate only in a limited number of cases. Those most in need of assistance are the last to seek it. Depression saps them of the energy they need to help themselves or to seek the help of others. All too often, people tragically surrender to despondency and take their own lives despite the best efforts of the churches, helping professions, and suicide prevention services.

Occasionally "feeling down" or "getting the blues" is

---

1. *The Uncommitted: Alienated Youth in American Society* (New York: Harcourt, Brace & World, 1965), p. 4.

the cost of being human. All of us have those times when life seems hopeless, when our problems seem overwhelming, when there appears to be nothing ahead in the tunnel but more tunnel. Some of us are more dominated by such feelings than others. Let's face it—there are optimists and there are pessimists—and no amount of analysis will ever explain away the differences.

In order to help others beat the blues, we should first recognize that there are contributing factors. Although such components cannot be strictly separated, it is helpful for purposes of discussion to characterize the following factors: circumstantial, personality, loss, lack, and fear.

Circumstantial Factors

Of all the factors that add to depression, circumstances are, relatively speaking, the easiest with which to deal. The counselor can effectively encourage a friend to change the circumstances of his or her life more readily than the counselor can help that friend change his or her personality. Some of the major circumstantial contributors to depression are:

Fatigue
Overcommitment
Overexcitement
Overanxiety
Improper diet
Lack of exercise
Illness
Improper environment
Change
Accomplishment
Success
Inconsistency

A great deal of depression is the body's natural reaction to circumstances. As such it will pass away, in large part, when conditions change. Simple friendly intervention that alters circumstance or elicits a change in circumstances can be of great benefit. For instance, let's consider intervening on behalf of a fatigued friend.

Responding to fatigue. Individuals tend to become depressed when they are overly tired as the result of too much work, too many worries, and too little sleep. When persons try to get their work done and meet personal responsibilities despite exhaustion, they usually make the situation worse. Efficiency drops; it takes a fatigued person several times as long to finish a task as well-rested persons. Circumstances are emotionalized—instead of doing the job at hand, the individual begins to complain about the job and co-workers, whine about the unfairness of life, feel unappreciated, and panic as the pressure to catch up mounts. Finally, the individual feels that the job is impossible, and, shortly thereafter, that life is hopeless. What should you do to help?

1. *Bring the real problem to the surface. Listen* to the complaints about fellow employees, the boss, the unsupportive family members, the demanding spouse, the unfairness and cruelty of life. *Don't argue.* Help your friend articulate the feelings, encouraging him or her to wallow in them if necessary. Have him or her *repeat* the whole story again. Repetition helps people sort out their feelings, look at themselves and their situation more clearly and rationally, and realize how much they are exaggerating and emotionalizing. Years ago, a lawyer told me that whenever clients came to him for advice about traumatic events in their lives, he always had them tell him everything twice. It was the second account that revealed to him whether he was dealing

with overstated emotional grievances or an actual legal dispute.

2. *Tell your friend, "I know how you must feel," and restate in your own words what you have heard.* Make sure that your restatement is as detailed as possible. Act as your friend's megaphone, making sure that the feelings are heard loud and clear. If necessary, supply what you have not been told with your own speculation about your friend's plight. Then encourage your friend to correct your account and *listen* to what your friend says. Once again, what you are doing is helping your friend *separate facts from feelings* so that he or she can hear his or her own fatigue and panic speaking. When your friend gains enough distance from the feelings, the facts will not appear so overwhelming and much of the depression will disappear.

3. *State what you have heard and seen.* Tell your friend that he or she is tired and cranky, and that his or her fatigue is like a Chinese finger lock—the more one struggles the tighter the grip. A tired person often needs to hear from a supportive individual that he or she looks tired and should do something about it—take an overdue vacation, take an afternoon off, go to a movie.

4. *Expect and ignore resistance.* When counseling a friend, be persistent. If a friend tells me I look tired, I will respond that I am fine. Besides, I don't have time to be tired. If a second friend tells me I look tired, I go look in the mirror to see if he is right. If a third friend says "You look tired," I leave work early and take a nap.

5. *Follow up.* Don't worry about appearing to be a nag. If your relationship as a caring friend has previously been established, your concern will be appreciated even if it does not seem so. All of us have a penchant for arguing with those who give us good

advice while silently paying much more attention to them than we would ever admit. As a matter of fact, each of us has an unconscious inclination to accept and follow advice—a tendency that salespeople, evangelists, and con artists manipulate, each in his or her own way.

6. *Try to negotiate an informal contract with your friend.* "You know that you are tired, that you are pushing yourself too hard, so if you want me to help you (by baby-sitting, cooking dinner, proofreading the manuscript), I want you to know that I am available. In any event, let's get together next week and see if you are getting the rest you need. Do you agree? If you start feeling panicky again, you phone me so we can talk it out. O.K.?" Such *simple contracts* with *definite responsibilities* and *time limits* are extremely valuable tools in all forms of counseling, whatever the problem may be.

7. *Keep your word.* If you promise to help, be sure to help. The last thing a depressed person needs is an inconsistent helper. Your efforts as a counselor should focus on the needs of the other person—not on making yourself feel good because someone indicates appreciation at your offer of help. A promise of help without follow-up is like a bad check. Not only is it worthless but it stirs up in the recipient a whole array of negative emotions—anger, disappointment, self-doubt, and distrust toward others. Excuses and apologies are poor substitutes for a dependable friend.

8. *Share who you are.* Depression is deepened by a loss of faith in the divine plan and purpose for one's life. Don't take advantage of your friend's pain by trying to sell him or her easy answers or theological nostrums. Be yourself, and as a Christian share with your friend who you are, to whom and what you are committed, and

your own sense of calling. Do not be ashamed to admit your doubts and failings, but gently and honestly restore your friend to a sense of being loved as a child of God and as your brother or sister in Christ.

With some of my clients who view life from a theistic perspective, I will suggest that we pray together or I will accept their invitation—even though their theology is a light year removed from mine. Resist the temptation to think that because you have prayed together about your friend's need you have turned your friend over to God and are no longer responsible. Prayer should deepen our commitments to one another, not abrogate them.

This description of intervening in the problem of a friend who is depressed due to fatigue is meant as a model for responding to all forms of depression and with many other difficulties as well. The steps are as follows:

1. Listen; listen again
2. Restate; listen yet again
3. Describe and prescribe
4. Ignore resistance
5. Follow up
6. Negotiate
7. Keep your word
8. Share who you are

Responding to overcommitment. Overcommitment results from an inability to say no. In order to be accepted and liked, we will agree to do much more than we can possibly do. We will commit resources of time, money, and caring as though they were limitless. When those to whom the commitments have been made place demands on us, the resources may prove inadequate. It is much easier to say, "I love you," than to be loving when your love is required. It is easier to volunteer to help with the Christmas bazaar than to make Christmas tree ornaments. It is simpler to use credit cards than to cover the bills.

When it comes time to pay the piper—to honor one's commitments—it is not always possible. Many of the best pipers I know are paupers! Not being able to respond, not being able to be everywhere that one should be, do everything that is expected, put all the promised checks in the mail, take care of business and family and friends and loved ones is downright depressing.

When prescribing remedies to overcommitment, concentrate on distinguishing between necessary obligations and self-imposed burdens. Encourage overloaded individuals to make a detailed, written list of all the demands on their time, money, and emotions. Take one at a time and ask, "Does this particular demand have to be met at this time? At all?"

Much depression results from "all or nothing" thinking—the attempt to resolve every concern at once, to cut the Gordian knot of distress and somehow find a solution for everything. When such magic resolutions are not forthcoming or attempted remedies fail to work, the individual's hopes for the future are dashed and the depression is only deepened. As a counselor, never indulge in the pursuit of magic "one size fits all" answers. Slowly and patiently, help your friend unravel the knot.

Financial overextension is as demoralizing as any form of overcommitment, so let's use it as an example. When a family or a business can no longer meet financial obligations, there are forms of protection available to them in federal and state bankruptcy laws.

One of the following strategies may be chosen: (1) ask the court to liquidate their assets, pay some of their debts, and discharge them from the remaining liabilities; (2) submit a reorganization plan that allows them, under court supervision, to repay some or most of their obligations over a number of months; or (3) negotiate an informal arrangement with their creditors to pay what they owe over a number of months. It is always better to take control of a bad financial situation and correct it for oneself through one of these strategies than to live with the endless uncertainty and anxiety of fiscal overcommitment.

The advantages of adopting any of the three financial strategies are *the restoration of a sense of control over one's life, an elimination of harassment, a lessening of one's sense of guilt, and a decrease in anxiety and depression.* Helping a friend arrive at a plan for fiscal solvency or for balancing the emotional demands on his or her personal life or for managing his or her time will have exactly the same results. When counseling an overcommitted friend, remember to listen, listen again, restate, listen yet again, describe and prescribe, ignore resistance, persist, negotiate, follow up, and share who you are.

Responding to excitement and anxiety. Depression often follows prolonged anxiety or excitement. At some point, the nervous system is unable to process any further data and damps down its ability to respond. In such cases, respond to the anxiety or the need for stimulation first. (See chapter 15, "Responding to Anxiety.") Describe it to your friend. Bring it out into the open. Confront it. Suggest alternatives. If you have witnessed the pattern of stress-overload-collapse in the past, anticipate that it will happen again and "describe and prescribe" before your friend hits bottom.

Responding to improper diet and environment. When I
served as executive director of mental health associations in Delaware and California, I was responsible for
the supervision of rehabilitation centers for the
resocialization of former mental patients. Included in
the schedule of activities were regular meals and snacks.
I noticed that our clients, most of whom were heavily
meditated, consumed enormous amounts of coffee
with cream and sugar, donuts, cake, cookies, and
chocolate candy. They also smoked heavily. Although I
am neither a medical doctor nor a nutritionist, I have
long suspected that consumption of caffeine, sugar,
bleached flour, and tobacco is a formula for depression.

I remember clients who were members of a contro-
versial sectarian organization and were subpoenaed to
appear in court in a conservatorship hearing. Their
parents were attempting to prove that they were
incapacitated, unable to care for their own needs. The
religious group wanted them to appear alert and in
control of their faculties. The hearing was scheduled
for late morning. After breakfast, the sect's leader gave
the recruits ice cream cones covered with bits of
chocolate candy, which they thought rather strange at
the time. During the hearing, they were attentive and
hyperactive. Later they told me that shortly after the
court proceedings, they felt empty, depleted, lethargic,
and depressed. The artificial high induced by a sudden
sugar infusion had quickly burned itself out, leaving
them fatigued and apathetic.

Improper diet, lack of exercise, and illness contribute
to depression. A psychologist with whom I have worked
for years tells her depressed clients to adopt some form
of physical exercise. She says, "I don't know why, but
doing anything, once a day, to the point of perspiration
is as effective in the treatment of depression as any form

of therapy." And, of course, when a person is sick, physical ennui readily blends with emotional languor.

Other circumstantial culprits include an environment lacking in proper ventilation, heating, and lighting, or one characterized by noise pollution. I have a friend who is the "Johnny Appleseed" of proper fluorescent lighting. He contends that lighting that closely resembles sunlight is exhilarating, but that most indoor lighting is depressing. At his insistence, I replaced the fluorescent tubes in the fixtures in my counseling and administrative offices. Other depression-retardants are classical music, the sounds of a wood fire, gently cascading water, the ocean, the songs of birds, and other natural sounds. Aquariums and natural history museums frequently sell excellent commercial recordings which create a serene mood, free of anxiety and depression. Whether or not changing the indoor lighting truly lifted the spirits of my depressed clients or their sometimes apathetic counselor, I cannot say, although I did note a decline in eye strain and fatigue. The point is that many depressing circumstances can be changed and the accompanying ennui diminished.

As a friend and adviser, be alert to such considerations as possible contributors to melancholy moods. If they are the culprits, work with your friend to bring under control those which can readily be changed. For example, set up a regimen of regular exercise; perhaps you and your friend can go for long walks together or join an exercise club.

Change, accomplishment, success. Virtually any major change in a person's circumstances—either for better or worse—can trigger states of depression. For example, a change of location can be profoundly disorienting. As the result of a move of even a few miles, one's entire support system can be disrupted. Friends and relatives are no longer available. Comfortable routines of grocery shopping, mail delivery, and transportation are disturbed. The problem is compounded when families are relocated from one side of the continent to another. Loneliness, uncertainty, unfamiliarity, and confusion as to one's identity and vocation are unavoidable.

About eleven years ago, my wife and I moved from Delaware to California so that I could accept a new job. To this day I am grateful to the new friends and co-workers who told me how to get to work and where to open a checking account and identified the local churches, restaurants, shopping malls, dentists, physicians. My dealing with California culture shock after thirty-five years in the Midwest and East reminded my wife, a native of northern California, of her coping during her two years in Delaware. For years I felt like a visitor from another planet. Today I feel that way when I visit my former environs. Every Christmas season I still have moments of nostalgia for the Chicago of my childhood and the Philadelphia/New Jersey of my early adulthood. Such moments last until I see the first scenes of winter snowstorms broadcast on television!

Even though I wanted to be in California so badly that I cried with joy on the airplane, and although I have found California to be a better environment for my life and work than anywhere else I have lived or visited, I am still an alien (as are most Californians). Neil Diamond expresses the sense well in his song, "I Am I Said." And such a sense of homelessness, the product of any major change in one's life, contributes to depression.

Success can be as profoundly depressing as failure. For success brings change and loss of direction. My friend Carl had a decade-long goal, getting his doctorate. When he attained it, it was as if he no longer had anything to live for. He had confused who he was with getting what he wanted. He also had attached false expectations to earning his degree. He thought that he would be financially secure, respected, and happy. Instead he found that his struggle for tenure had just begun, that his neighbors had little conception of what a Ph.D. in psychology was all about and were jealous of his light work schedule and abundant vacations. He discovered that in the real world without subsidized student housing and health care, his assistant professor's salary left him with less discretionary income than had his meager stipend as a graduate assistant. And now that he had time to spend with his wife and children, he learned to his chagrin that he had little talent for the role of husband or father.

The only thing that can offset the effects of major change is a "personal safety zone," a fixed point of reference—something in a person's life that is dependable, trustworthy, and consistent. On a spiritual level, this requires faith in a caring and just God. On a psychological level, persons need to have a sense of who they are and what their commitments and vocation are. On a personal level, there must be someone whom we can trust, whose love for us is constant and secure. The counselor can help but can never fully take up the slack. Ultimately, all of us must decide for ourselves what we believe, to what ends our life is directed, to whom we are committed, and whom we may trust. The role of supportive, caring friends is as important in the process of establishing a personal "safety zone" as any influence. The essential ingredient for establishing a sense of security amidst change and turmoil is having

someone who is always there for us. The consistency of
the counselor can be the bedrock of a friend's personal
security. And conversely, an inconsistent counselor,
who professes concern but is not truly committed to the
individual pours salt into the wounds. The last thing
that an insecure or discouraged person needs is more
inconsistency.

Personality Factors

When my son was an infant, I used to throw him a few
inches into the air and catch him. It was a form of play
that he loved. When my daughter was the same age, I
discovered that this kind of play terrified her. Individuals are individuals—alike in certain respects yet
frustratingly different from birth.

Depressed individuals are overwhelmingly preoccupied with themselves. Some are shy; others painfully
self-conscious; still others incredibly sensitive to criticism; some all of the above. Some depressed persons are
almost inarticulate. They seem to lack either the energy
or the ability to communicate in anything other than
crestfallen gazes and sighs. Others talk too much. They
gripe, complain, wail, and moan. They don't really
converse; they wait for the other person to fall silent so
they can continue talking about themselves. They have
a tendency to talk incessantly, as though interminable
discussion of a problem is the same as resolving it.

Depressed persons feel disconnected, alone, aloof,
cut off, and shunned. They are lonely in any crowd,
alienated despite any approval shown them. As we have
noted, they are often "all or nothing" thinkers. If things
are not entirely as they want them, completely under
control, they feel like total failures. They are other-

directed, looking for happiness not in self-satisfaction but in living up to the expectations of others.

Depression-prone individuals are overly sensitive to stimuli. They experience higher highs and deeper lows. They are more impatient, more prone to take offense, more easily bruised by unintended insults, more afraid of taking chances. When they are down, they are so emotionally exhausted and unresponsive that they do not feel very much at all.

Individuals who are inclined to be depressed have trouble tolerating ambiguity. They are comfortable with clear, black or white situations. They want easy answers, self-evident formulas that cover all difficult situations. They have a love for clichés, proverbs, and platitudes. Since neither the world nor the people with whom they are involved are totally trustworthy, dependable, or consistent, the traditional rules seem to cover fewer and fewer of life's circumstances. Not being able to discern whom to trust or to know in what to believe, throws such individuals into consternation, confusion, and brooding. Their simplistic world views set them up as ready victims of their own false expectations. Their other-directedness leaves them easy marks for manipulators and scoundrels.

It has often been observed that depressed persons are filled with misdirected, suppressed anger. Instead of turning their rage upon their real or supposed tormenters, they psychologically beat themselves up instead. The observer can account for this tendency by saying that some people (females, ethnic minorities, fat children, short children), were raised to sublimate their anger and accept rationalizations about their need to respect their betters or elders or those more deserving of love and attention than they. The unexpressed anger corrodes the individual's self-esteem and evokes a sense of helplessness. Does depression result from lacking a sense of control over one's life or does the sense of lack of control over one's life arise from the depression? It is difficult to tell.

When responding to the way a person is, the counselor must begin by accepting him. The counselor's attitude should be, at the outset of the relationship, acceptance of the person and indifference toward the person's inclinations. Some people are more depressed or depression-prone than others, but a person *has* such tendencies—such tendencies are not *who they are*. A person has traits but he or she is more than traits. If I have a cold, no one judges me to be a cold person. If I have a broken leg, they do not assess the real me to be broken as well. All of us are more complex, valuable, and significant than any condition we may have—even when that condition is a constituent of our basic personality.

The basic formula is: support the person and remain strictly neutral toward his or her traits. Begin by affirming the person for what is valuable to you—his or her sense of humor, talents, vocabulary, responsiveness, dependability, the way he or she hugs, whatever. There are few individuals who, just as they are, cannot make me feel alive, human, valuable, if I allow myself to feel. If you cannot find one feature of value in a person, then concentrate on the potential that is hiding before your eyes. (Yes. Potential can be very, very well concealed!)

Maintain strict neutrality toward the traits that concern you. When you have proven yourself a caring person, you will have an opportunity to lure your friend toward acceptable behavior and away from undesirable behavior. Judicious reinforcement of desirable behavior coupled with the example of others within

a supportive community can work miracles of transformation.

However, there are bounds even to the patience of a
saint. There is a time for gentle persuasion and there is
time for direct encounter. Some problems simply
cannot be ignored and some solutions seem so obvious
that the counselor cannot resist insisting on them. But
the right to confront a person must be earned. A
relationship of mutual respect and caring must be
established. More harm has been caused on earth by
unsolicited advice than by all the legions of hell. An
acquaintance of mine, who is a minister, has established
such a reputation for tactless, inconsiderate, and
inappropriate intervention that many of his parishioners would gladly pay him to keep his advice to himself.

If you find it impossible to establish a nonjudgmental
counseling role, remind yourself that you weren't
always so lovable yourself and that while you were yet
helpless, hopeless, and obnoxious, God showed his love
for you and sent his Son to die for you (Rom. 5:6-8).
Similarly, if it were not for the unmerited favor that has
been showered on you by those who have loved you, you
would be less of a person than you are today. I know
that when I deliberately focus on the unconditional love
I have received, I am far more willing to overcome my
apathy, aversion, and antipathy toward others.

If you remain stymied, uncomfortable, and anxious,
then withdraw, get out of the way, and let someone else
help. You are not the only soldier in God's army. Being
alert and responsive to the needs of others does not
obligate you to personally solve all the world's problems. If you are convinced that you cannot help
a particular person or deal with a particular problem,
find someone who can. Wise counselors recognize their
limitations.

Loss—Termination

Depression is a common reaction to a sudden change in one's self-image. We all tend to confuse our sense of who we are with the answer to questions such as, "What do you do for a living?" and "Are you married or single?" When there is a loss of any significant factor by which we know and identify ourselves, pain, confusion, and depression are not far behind. Among the most ordinary losses and their causes are the following:

Loss	*Cause*
Relationships	Death, divorce, changed circumstances
Career	Retirement, dismissal, disability
Health	Illness
Financial security	Economic change, poor investments, fraud
Self-esteem	Failure
Control	Frustration
Faith	Disappointed expectations, misconceptions

When individuals undergo major changes in their lives or lose something basic to their self-conception, there is inevitable confusion, dread, and panic. A friend of mine is going through a divorce that he is desperately resisting. He became disoriented and lost his way home from the shopping center, which is only a half mile from his house. A thirty-six-year-old friend became deeply depressed when the youngest of her five children started school. She felt that she was no longer needed. A novelist, experiencing memory lapses in his early sixties, became deeply morose, convinced that he would never write again. Another friend, who had lost the vision in one eye, committed suicide because he believed that he would end up totally blind and dependent on other people.

The counselor's task in responding to loss is to lead the friend through a natural grieving/healing process. Elisabeth Kübler-Ross relates the stages through which the terminally ill pass after being informed of their condition. She describes denial, isolation, anger, bargaining, depression, and, finally, acceptance. All profound shocks to our sense of identity and security elicit similar responses. When a marriage ends, the psychological aftermath incorporates anger, rage, sadness, depression, a deep sense of guilt and personal failure, shame, regret, fear and distrust of the formerly beloved, nostalgia, the desire for reconciliation, a confused sense of identity or ego boundaries, self-justification, and, ultimately, acceptance and coping. The supportive friend listens, sympathizes, and points to the hopeful future that he or she sees in the distance.

What can you do when friends are trying to cope with loss?

1. *Insist that your friends accept the facts of the situation.* Make sure that they know that you are available and that they are not alone. Encourage your friends to vent the anger they feel toward the unfairness of the circumstances, the duplicity of other persons, whatever. Much that surfaces will be exaggerated and unfair. For instance, someone will become enraged with a dead spouse even though the death was through no fault of that person. The "guilty party" in a divorce will accuse the other party of behavior that never happened. Do not argue at this stage. Create a supportive, secure environment in which your friends can ventilate their

feelings. If you sense that anger or sadness are being choked back, ask your friends how they are feeling, tell them how you would feel, cite analogies from your own experience. Don't be surprised if you, at times, end up on the receiving end of their stored up rage.

2. *When your friends begin to bargain, to suggest totally unrealistic scenarios for responding to the situation, stop sympathizing and begin describing the facts as you see them.* Tell the truth gently, lovingly, humbly, and in the first person. Use such "I statements" as, "I may be wrong but what I feel about your loss is. . . ." or "I know that if I were in your shoes I would want. . . ." Point out the exaggerations, inconsistencies, and unreasonable expectations of what your friends have been telling you. If appropriate, suggest that your friends have not owned up to their responsibilities or that they are accepting too much blame.

3. *When grief and depression settle in, you can provide two important functions: being there and pointing to the future.* When someone close to me died a few years ago, the grief was so intense that I did not think I could survive. A rabbi told the mourners that even though we probably would not believe him the pain would be less with each passing day, that God had arranged things so that we would in time "forget" our loved ones so that we could bear the pain of losing them. Something in his words gave me hope. I do not believe that I have lost the memory of one minute spent with my loved one, but the pain did diminish, and, eventually, fade away. His confident prediction of the future pulled me just the slightest bit out of my immediate trauma. It was a start.

Lack

Similar to depression caused by loss is that occasioned by lack or frustration. To *lose* something, the individual has to have it in the first place. To *lack* something is to sense that something is absent from one's life, or is present in too limited an amount. A few garden-variety frustrations are caused by the following:

Lack of hope
Lack of direction
Lack of appreciation
Lack of love
Lack of desire
Lack of resources
Lack of control
Lack of self-esteem

A lack can be real or psychological. If your friend lacks something tangible, give it to him or her or help him or her get it. Such lacks or insufficiencies rarely cause depression, but an inner sense of lack is every bit as painful as a sense of loss and is even more frustrating to deal with. The passage of time and a change in circumstances heals most losses, but all the appreciation or love in the world cannot assuage a self-centered complaint of not being appreciated or loved enough. How much is enough?

A friend of mine lost the ability to play the violin as the result of the amputation of a finger. Even before the loss, he lacked the ability to play in a symphony orchestra. The lack caused him no pain; he had no desire to be a professional violinist. But suppose he had retained his finger and had desired above all else to be a concert violinist. The lack of talent could have been much more depressing than the loss of the finger actually was.

The sense of lacking something is often the expression of one's fantasy of who one is and what one should possess. Since what one lacks exists primarily in fantasy, it can best be provided by fantasy. Encourage your friend to daydream. In the most concrete terms, have your friend describe what it would be like if all wishes could be fulfilled. Elaborate and expand this reverie. One of three things will happen: (1) playing with the fantasy will become engrossing and entertaining, (2) your friend will suddenly laugh at how preposterous the fantasy is, and (3) the fantasy will transform itself into a plan of action. In any event, the depression will disappear.

Fear

Fear of failure and disappointment can be paralyzing, so can fear of success. By allowing self-doubt to moor us to the comfortable present we know, we are spared the future we do not know. No matter how unsatisfactory circumstances may be, the self of today is stable and amicable, but that self that might change and take risks is unknown and frightening. To want more, to sense that there has to be more, but to be afraid to pursue it leaves us open to frustration and depression.

Let your friends know that they are loved, appreciated, and respected just as they are. Nothing will more forcefully empower them to take a chance on what they could be than your affirmation of them as they are. Then lure them into the fantasy game.

RESPONDING TO DEPRESSION

What Works?—A Summary

Indulgence. By loving your friends, you enable them to love themselves.

Distraction. Entertaining your friends and amplifying their dreams get them out of their emotional rut.

Motivation. Planning, predicting, sharing dreams breaks the emotional logjam and creates a vision of a hopeful future.

Service. Encourage your friends to use their talents and abilities to serve others, even if all that they can do is serve meals at a skid row mission. Depression is rooted in preoccupation with one's self. Turning attention to others breaks its hold.

Community. Help your friends find others who share the same interests and values. There are limits to what persons can do for themselves and what you can do for them.

Realistic expectations. Help your friends sort out what is possible, what is not. Call attention through the use of "I statements" to unrealistic tendencies in their thinking. Do they blame others for their problems? Do they exaggerate their condition? Do they play martyr? Do they frequently fall into "all or nothing" thinking? Are they generally naïve about the way people are and the way the world works?

Self-awareness, self-direction. Help your friends evaluate and appreciate who they are and who they can be.

Humor. Don't lose your own sense of humor and don't be afraid to use humor to illumine your friend's dilemma.

Time. Remind your friend of the simple wisdom of the bumper sticker that says: "Time heals all wounds and wounds all heels!"

Renewing faith. Depression represents a loss of faith. See suggestions for sharing faith in chapters 5 and 6.

Restoring control. Helping a friend restore control in even a small aspect of his or her life can wipe out the sense of powerlessness that is so typical of depression. I recently helped a friend, who was going through a time of uncertainty about his future, clean out his clothes closets—a half day's job. The end result was more space, a large donation to Goodwill, the discovery of several perfectly wearable shirts and slacks that had been lost in the pandemonium, many therapeutic "walks down memory lane" as a given garment about to be discarded triggered memories and emotions, and a general feeling on the part of my friend that he could get other aspects of his life under control with or without assistance.

Acceptance of oneself. Learn, and instill in others, the Serenity Prayer of Alcoholics Anonymous:

> God grant us serenity to accept the
>   things we cannot change
> Courage to change the things we can
> And wisdom to know the difference.

Expressing anger. Give your friend permission to express his rage and teach him how anger may be made productive. (See chapter 9, "Anger and Forgiveness.")

Shock. When all else fails, and you run out of understanding and compassion, and you are sick of seeing the same forlorn countenance, tell your friend exactly how you feel. Sometimes it takes the counselor's anger to shock a depressed individual back into contact with reality.

C H A P T E R   15

Responding to Anxiety

Case Notes: *Adrienne*

Adrienne was a faculty member at a vocational high school. She was always well groomed and fastidiously dressed. She taught typing and transcription and was highly regarded by her peers and supervisors. Her teaching credential was temporary because she had not yet earned her bachelor's degree. She had been taking courses for eight years, had more than enough credit hours, but her grade point average was just below the requirement for graduation. All she needed was a grade of C or better in any course. Each time she took a final examination, she froze and wrote nothing. The result would be another D or F.

Marie

Marie's husband was transferred by his company to northern California. They found a new house, enrolled their children in school, and quickly made new friends. One day, Marie noticed that she was afraid to drive to the supermarket. She didn't know why. She had driven there often enough during the past few months. She began to be terribly anxious about her children's safety. She asked them to play at home after school and on weekends. She stopped attending PTA and playing tennis. Soon she would not leave her house.

"I have this sense of doom," she explained. "I just know that if I leave the house or let the children leave the house, something awful will happen."

Tom

Tom was a lonely graduate student. He met Shamma in the stacks of the university library. She was the illegitimate child of an Indian mother and a Greek father. After several chance meetings at the library, he asked her out for a drive. It was the first of many afternoon outings—to the zoo, to movies, to restaurants, to the azalea gardens in the park. One day, she asked him, "What do you want of me?" He replied, "I've come to love you."

He drove her home. Each searched the face of the other for a long moment before they parted, but he never saw her again. He was too afraid.

The New Testament teaching on anxiety may be summarized in two sentences: (1) *do not* be afraid—stop fearing what you should not fear—and (2) *do* be afraid—start fearing what you should fear. *Do not be afraid!* When angels speak to human beings (Matt. 1:20; 28:5; Luke 1:13, 30; 2:10; Acts 27:24), or Jesus speaks to his amazed disciples after some awesome display of his power, the first words spoken are "do not be afraid" (or in the language of the King James version, "Fear not," Matt. 14:27). When his hearers are more concerned with food, shelter, and clothing than about the kingdom of God, the teaching of Jesus is clear: Don't be afraid. Don't worry about such things. Seek first God's kingdom and righteousness and let God take care of the rest (Matt. 6:33; Luke 12:31). And, says Jesus, don't borrow trouble: "Do not worry about tomorrow, for tomorrow will worry about itself;

enough for the day is its own evil" (Matt. 6:34 LDS). However, Jesus also issued this "good news/bad news" warning to his disciples: "Stop being afraid of those who kill the body, but who are not able to kill the soul; but be afraid rather of the one who is able both soul and body to destroy on the garbage heap" (Matt. 10:28 LDS).

Jesus was not a Pollyanna; he was a proclaimer of priorities. Don't be afraid of what can't really hurt you, he maintained, but respect what really can. It is like saying, "Don't be afraid of matches, but don't let your children play with them." Jesus knew that how much money you have beyond what you need for survival, how many friends you have beyond those whose faith supports your own, how many clothes hang in your closet, whatever you own or control, whatever other people think of you are things that ultimately make no difference. Get your priorities straight, Jesus insisted.

The biblical teaching is to give everyone and everything the respect that they deserve—and no more. Thus Christians are instructed to obey the law, honor legitimate government, pay taxes, and live peaceably with all other people (Rom. 13:1-7). Give each person his or her just due, be as respectful of the feelings of others as you would have others be of yours, but don't get so hung up in making a living and dealing with other people that you forget who you are, to whom you belong, and to whom you are ultimately responsible. Respect everyone to whom respect is due, but don't be awestruck by anyone. Ultimately, the only one we should fear is God, Jesus demanded.

When I was a college student, it was common to refer to the first half of the twentieth century as "the age of anxiety," which suggests that previous ages were tranquil. They weren't. Our grandparents may not have worried about nuclear war and environmental pollution but the threat of death, war, famine, and disease, the scourge of poverty, and the misery caused by wrong decisions and ill fortune were just as frightening to them as to us today. Perhaps their fears were realistic and ours more self-indulgent and neurotic. Perhaps we are more anxious than they because we are more concerned about intangibles such as ego-gratification, sexual fulfillment, meaningful relationships, personal happiness, and individual freedom. Since people do not know what any of these terms mean, they never feel that they have attained enough of any of them. No wonder we are anxious. Perhaps ours is an age of anxiety because we are without transcendent moorings, spiritual perspective, and moral certainties. Thus, it is much more difficult for us to feel at home in the universe than it was for our forebears. A person who does not know the rules of the game is always anxious.

Whether we are any more anxious today than we were in the past, I cannot say. But one thing is sure: there is always more than enough anxiety to go around. Anxiety is exhausting, confining, and, finally, destructive. An hour or two of uncertainty, of worrying about things over which one has no control, of mentally wrestling with what might have been or what yet might be leaves one more drained than eight hours of hard physical labor. When people are anxious, they either cannot find the words to communicate with others or they talk too fast, too loud, and too much. In either case, the other person has no idea what the anxious one wants or needs. Anxiety sets the body at war against itself, consuming itself with illness and dysfunctions. The susceptibility to virtually every debilitating, disabling, and life-threatening disease is increased by persistent anxiety.

Anxiety distorts our perceptions of others, causing us to suspect their motives, distrust their commitments, harm their interests as well as our own. Although greed in the form of expansionism causes its share of conflicts between nations, the inability to tolerate the anxiety of ambiguous political situations triggers far more.

Anxiety is both inherited and created by circumstances. Some individuals are *born anxious*. They are more sensitive to stimuli, more prone to overreact, and more fearful than others. (Some infants seem heedless of personal danger; others are pathetically timorous.) They are what they are. Others *become anxious* because they are reared by overprotective parents, because they are denied adequate nurturing, because their home lives are chaotic and confused, because too much is demanded of them too soon. Firstborn and only children are notoriously anxious. They are overrepresented in any list of achievers as well as in the client rolls of psychiatrists.

Finally, all of us, from time to time, *have anxiety thrust upon us*. Anxiety is our general reaction to stressful stimuli. It is the body's way of preparing for "fight or flight." We are afraid of being hurt—physically and emotionally. We fear what we do not know—strangers, change, the depths of our own psyches. We are afraid of repeating the mistakes of the past. We are afraid that if we try something new, we will fail. We are afraid of not being able to pay our bills, of not being able to maintain our standard of living, of not being able to care for ourselves when we are old. We are even afraid of succeeding, for success requires change, forces us to deal with options and opportunities for which we may find ourselves unprepared.

We worry about our jobs, our spouses, our children, our relatives; we worry about what others think of us,

whether the stranger on the subway will mug us,
whether the government is telling us the truth, what will
happen to us if we do what we want to, what will happen
if we do not do what we want to. We worry about our
health, our weight, the substances "they" are putting in
the food we eat, the water we drink, and the air we
breathe. We worry about whether our appearance is
youthful enough, whether our clothes are clean
enough, our glassware spotless enough, our breath
fresh enough, our body odors inoffensive, and whether
or not the home team will win the Super Bowl.

Most of the time, we endure, we immerse ourselves in
our work or our families, and somehow we manage. At
other times, the intensity of our fears gets turned up
past the point of endurance. We become so overwhelmed by our chronic self-doubts and uncertainties
that we become indecisive and faltering. Even thinking
of what we want fills us with dread, with a sense of
impending doom. Or the immediate stress overcomes
us and we panic; our sleep is disturbed; we become
paralyzed with fear; we become hysterical and out of
control. In these moments, our fears make cowards of
us all. We become our own worst enemies. We become
isolated and incoherent—beyond the help or reach of
others. We may even become violent or self-destructive.
Or the anxiety may burn up all of our capacity to cope,
leaving us exhausted and depressed.

Lurking behind all anxiety is lack of faith. Anxious
persons are those who cannot believe in themselves, in
the order and dependability of their world, in the
trustworthiness of other human beings, or in the
ultimate justice of God. In the New Testament, *the
opposite of anxiety is faith.* In the Gospels, faith is the spark
without which the healing, revivifying power of God
cannot be ignited. It is through the faith of those who
seek him that Jesus restores the infirm and raises the

dead. On the basis of the faith of the supplicant, Jesus heals both those who ask for his help for themselves and those who beseech him for help for others. It is the insufficiency of faith that annuls his power. For example, if Peter had not been of such "little faith," he could have walked with Jesus on the waves. In the Revelation of John, chief among the characteristics of those consigned to the lake of fire are cowardice and lack of faith (Rev. 21:8).

To paraphrase the biblical message: the things that we fear may be worth fearing, but the world goes on whether we worry or not. However, an attitude of fearfulness reflects a loss of grounding in the fundamental realities that sustain us; such lack of perspective can eventually destroy us. The primary task of counseling anxious persons is to help them recover their faith—their sense that their world is meaningful, that it supports their aspirations and efforts, that their inner resources are adequate for the challenges of the present and the unpredictable contingencies of the future.

HINTS FOR COUNSELING ANXIOUS FRIENDS

1. *Listen; listen again; and advise.* Follow the guidelines suggested elsewhere in this book. Remember that anxiety distorts communication, making it harder for anxious persons both to understand others and to express their feelings and needs.

2. *Keep the faith—but not to yourself.* Basic, existential anxiety is caused by lack of meaning. Meaninglessness, in turn, is the state of not belonging to an ordered, moral universe. Without faith in a divine plan for humankind and a purpose for each life, the individual's

few years of existence become insignificant, inconsequential, and absurd. It is from the ultimate ground of being that our sense of responsibility derives, and it is from this sense that we obtain the notion of freedom. For where there is no freedom, there can be no responsibility; and without responsibility, we have no motivation except the satisfaction of our immediate urges.

Through faith in the divine-human partnership in the ongoing creative process, each life becomes significant. Through faith, we transcend the pettiness, unfairness, and caprice of everyday existence. Without faith in the ultimate judgment of God, we are left at the mercy of impersonal forces, blind chance, and our own foibles. Faith in the mercy and justice of God points us beyond the distress of the present toward the imminent reign of righteousness. Faith does not protect the believer against suffering; it is the source of hope and courage in the midst of suffering.

Does life make sense? Perhaps it does and perhaps it does not. But living as if it makes sense means living with an awareness of self-worth and dignity. Living as if there is neither purpose nor direction reduces the individual to the level of an animal without resources, to an existence full of insecurity and terror. For when the everyday world becomes a jungle, everyone becomes an enemy, threatening the individual's survival and well-being.

So share your faith; enhance your friends' sense of purpose, order, and hope.

3. *Practice disinhibition.* The best way to deal with fears is to confront them. A useful approach is to plan a program that divides the performance of a dreaded activity into a number of small, manageable steps. For instance, if one's friends are afraid of flying, drive them to a nearby airport. Spend the day watching airplanes

take off and land. Get permission from an airline to show your friends around an airplane (on the ground, of course). Take them into the cockpit and introduce them to the crew so that the crew may explain the various controls and instruments. At regular intervals, have your friends share their reactions with you and with those you meet at the airport. The next time you take a trip by airplane video tape it or take several dozen photographs detailing the entire process. Show the material to your friends, telling them item by item about the experience.

Have your friends simulate the experience with you as you sit together in their office or living room. Have them describe their imaginary plane ride to you in detail. After each detail, have them practice a relaxation technique such as the comfort zone. (See suggestions 11 and 12 below.) Try to focus on the aspect of the experience that is causing the greatest apprehension. Is it the lack of control that bothers them? The fear of heights? The fear of motion sickness? Ask how they have conquered similar fears in the past. Look for the step-by-step tactics that they consciously or unconsciously used then. Have them describe those past successes to you at each step in your current process.

Introduce them to as many people as possible who have overcome the same fear. Encourage them to discuss their common experiences. Buy tickets for the shortest scheduled flight from the nearest airport. Divide the experience into the short, rehearsed stages that you have practiced together, employing a relaxation technique at the beginning of each stage. Board the plane together. Encourage your friends to talk themselves through the experience, relating to you what is occurring, how it reminds them of the simulations, how they feel. Reassure them by reminding them of previous successes and by urging them to return to their comfort zone or relaxation technique.

Many fears (e.g. fear of public speaking, fear of leaving one's home, fear of heights, fear of driving) can be aided by a similar program of disinhibition.

4. *Confront all myths.* Anxieties are fueled by prejudices, misconceptions, exaggerations, and false expectations. Get them out into the open and confront them. A judicious use of wit and irony can be extremely useful.

5. *Accentuate the positive; eliminate the negative.* Anxious persons overestimate negative factors and ignore the positive. As a friend, your appraisal of the anxiety-causing situation can reverse the picture. Don't appear argumentative. Adopt the "devil's advocate" stance: "Well, you know your situation better than I do. But just for the sake of argument, I'm going to take the opposite point of view. Let's see if we can look at this situation in another way."

A similar approach is to ask your friends to answer this question in detail, What's the worst that can happen? No matter what they reply ask the question again. To their next reply, ask once more.

6. *Establish rules; set limits.* Help your friends determine their own guidelines. Ask them what they want to accomplish in the present situation, what their plans are for doing it, and how they will measure success or failure. Setting limits is particularly important. If such and such happens by next Monday, then I will do *x*. If such and such does not happen by next Monday, then I will do *y*. For example, let's say that John is feeling insecure about his relationship to Mary. He wonders how she really feels about him, but he is afraid to ask for fear that she will spurn him. So you and he agree to the following rule or limit: if Mary does not tell John how she feels by this next birthday, he will ask her. By

removing the open-endedness from the situation, the anxiety is significantly reduced.

Also missing from the lives of many anxious persons is a sense of moral absolutes. Without rules and standards of behavior, individuals are at the mercy of the whims of the moment. Often they are left feeling bewildered and apprehensive as a pet does when its owners move into a new home. Have your friends review their personal dos and don'ts. Ask them what behavior of theirs would cause them the greatest sense of shame. Ask them to express why. Explore what makes them feel guilty. Does their guilt spring from their own sense of who they are, who they want to be, and the kind of world in which they want to live or does it arise from family programming and social conditioning that they intellectually reject?

7. *Be prepared.* The more thorough one's preparation for a stressful situation, the more comfortable the performance. The trick is to reduce the fearful impending event to a script that can be memorized, rehearsed, and mastered. If your friends are afraid of an impending interview, pretend that you are the interviewer and run through test interviews with them until they are comfortable with the process. Always overdo it—conduct seven or eight mock interviews. Skills should not only be practiced; they should be overlearned.

I used to prepare for college examinations by getting some of my most anxious classmates together and teaching them how to answer the anticipated questions. By pretending to be the teacher in this relatively stressless circumstance, I was able to organize the material and prepare myself for the coming test. Because they had undergone these simulated exams, when the time came for the real thing, they were partially repeating a learned script and partially responding to the areas in which we had not correctly anticipated what the instructor would ask. Having the script gave the extra time to be inventive in the areas for which we had not prepared. Also the group sessions disinhibited us, familiarized us with the material, exposed us to one another's viewpoints and methods of organizing the material.

8. *Reinterpret anxiety as excitement.* Much anxiety is the body's reaction to new and challenging situations. Sometimes it is possible to welcome the fear, to interpret it as excitement rather than apprehension. In a sense, excitement is fear that is positively valued. For example, I am frightened when I watch a football game and the home team is behind by six points with less than a minute on the clock or when I ride a roller coaster, but I am not anxious. Help your friends welcome anxiety about coming events or present challenges.

9. *Discourage your friends from trying so hard.* When we try too hard to do something, our circuits overload. Imagine trying to thread a needle before a live audience on a television program. Your hands would probably shake uncontrollably. Relaxation techniques and preparation can convert your friends' deliberate actions into "performances." When your friends no longer concentrate on the action, the shakiness will disappear.

10. *Plan a vacation.* Give your friends permission to take a break from the problems that are overwhelming them. Take them to lunch. Encourage them to get away for a long weekend. If they have been postponing annual vacations for fear their businesses cannot get along without them (or for fear that they can!), insist that they take it now.

11. *Build a comfort zone.* A key to relaxing is having a precise image of a safe and secure place where one is unconditionally accepted. My comfort zone is my memory of my maternal grandmother. When I am

anxious, I mentally send myself back to my childhood and to her home in Maywood, Illinois. I recall the sights, sounds, odors of the old house and remember her reassuring tone of voice, and how it felt to relax with my head in her lap.

12. *Teach your friends to relax.* The return to the comfort zone is one technique. Other methods include: the relaxation response—alternately tensing tightly and relaxing fully one's muscles, group by group; counting down—intensely concentrating on one's breath, counting each inhalation and exhalation; repetition—repeating a group of words such as the Lord's Prayer or a collection of nonsense syllables again and again until one's consciousness is lost in them. Massage is an effective stress reducer. An hour with a trained masseur can be extremely helpful.

13. *Identify the most dangerous person in the world.* In his account of the est Training, Luke Rhinehart describes a group activity known as the "danger process" as follows:

We are all lying on the floor with our eyes closed. . . . We are being instructed to become actors . . . and pretend to be filled with fear, to be terrified of the person lying next to us. . . .

Then we are told to extend our fear to the people on all four sides of us—they are dangerous and fill us with fear. . . . Now everyone on our whole side of the room is dangerous and frightening. . . . Everyone in the whole room is out to kill us. . . . The whole city is our enemy and fills us with fear. . . . Everybody on earth is after us, they are *all* our enemies, they *all* frighten us. After a slow, repetitious buildup the whole room is filled with writhing, groaning, moaning, screaming, shrieking, crying. . . .

And at the very height of the dramatized fear the trainer quiets us enough so that his voice can be heard again over the din:

". . . the thing you ought to know is that the person lying beside you who you were afraid of. He is deathly afraid of *you*. And . . . the amazing truth is that everyone in this *room* is afraid, screaming, moaning, afraid of *you*. [Laughter is heard.] And finally, yes, you've got it, everyone on this whole planet that frightened you, everyone is actually deathly afraid of *you*. They're all afraid of you, *everybody*, and they always have been and always will be. Those people you never dare look at on elevators—they're afraid to look at *you*. [Laughter] . . . Those people whose eyes you don't meet when you're passing people in the street, they're . . . scared . . . of *you!* . . . And that boss who called you into the office the other day, he was frightened as hell, of *you* . . . they're all afraid of you."[1]

You are the most dangerous person in the world!

14. *Buy a pet.* Next to grandparents dogs and cats are the greatest natural therapists in the world. Pets offer unconditional acceptance, forgiveness, reciprocity, creature comfort, and entertainment. They remain with us as long as they live, which is frequently fourteen to eighteen years. They demand little, are always available, never threaten us with divorce, misunderstand us, or sue. Our interaction with them relaxes both us and them, so take your anxious friends to the nearest animal shelter or pet store.

15. *Scare them.* Take your friends to an amusement park and urge them to ride the attraction from which the most screams are emanating. Or take them to the latest Hollywood slasher or adventure movie. Being scared, in a controlled and time-limited manner, releases a great deal of the muscular tension the body stores.

16. *Advise reduction in caffeine and sugar consumption.*

---

1. Luke Rhinehart, *The Book of est* (New York: Holt, Rinehart & Winston, 1976), pp. 106-7. I have added the words, "You are the most dangerous person in the world!" because they were part of the "danger process" that I witnessed when I evaluated the est Training in 1983.

The physical effects of these two substances mimic and exaggerate anxiety. Also prescription stimulants and diet pills can cause extreme irritability and suspicion.

17. *Encourage regular exercise.* Take your friends for a daily one-mile walk. Both the activity and your attention will markedly lessen their fretfulness. Regular exercise helps discharge the stored-up muscular tension that accumulates in an anxious person.

18. *Give them a good laugh.* Comedy is also based on the excitation of tension and its subsequent release. Any good comedian or comic production mirrors our own anxieties, helps us gain a sense of perspective, encourages us to laugh at ourselves, and offers us temporary relief from our own tensions.

19. *Offer reassurance.* A hug and the words, "You can do it," are the greatest tranquilizer in the world.

CHAPTER 16

Marriage and Divorce

Case Notes: *Myron*

Myron is a successful attorney. He was president of a local Rotary club when we met. He had invited me to speak to the group. A week later, he and his wife had dinner with my wife and me. Myron's wife, Jolene, was twenty-two years his junior. She appeared totally enamored with him. I was a bit embarrassed by her constant displays of affection and her cloying baby talk, but they seemed to enjoy each other tremendously.

About three months later, I was surprised when Myron phoned me for "a professional appointment." When he arrived at my office, he appeared deeply upset. He paced incessantly as we talked. First, he told me about his first wife, Irma. "We were married for nearly twenty-five years. She is smarter than I am, always earned more money, is better known professionally, and when she divorced me, I agreed to pay alimony. I still am paying a third of what I make—but she was such a controlling bitch that I just had to get away from her. I would have given her anything."

He stopped pacing, sat down, and continued: "So now I'm married to Jolene. She was one of my clients. She was recovering from her first marriage that had just ended in divorce. She had been married to this abusive drunk.

I helped her regain a measure of self-confidence, and then she became totally dependent on me. She is so effusive, warm, and appreciative. She made me feel ten feet tall. It was so different from my marriage to Irma. It felt so wonderful. But you know what? It's getting old. Being married to someone who is completely dependent on you—someone who won't make the simplest decision without you, someone who hovers over you every minute—is just as draining as being married to a controlling bitch!"

Russell and Nadia

Russell and Nadia came to me for marriage counseling. When Russell, Nadia, and I were together, they both seemed to want their marriage to work and told me how frustrated they felt about the tensions that had developed between them. When I met separately with Russell, he made it clear that he was sick of Nadia and that he had fallen in love with another woman, Liza. When I met with Nadia, she communicated clearly and succinctly that she was tired of Russell's lack of enthusiasm for her and that she was well aware that there was another woman.

I asked Russell what he really wanted. He replied, "To dump Nadia and live with Liza." When I asked Nadia what she really wanted, she said, "I don't care. I would just as soon live alone as put up with this crap. As a matter of fact, I would be completely happy if Russell would leave." Finally, I got them together and told them the truth as I saw it: "Russell is no longer in love with you, Nadia. He would rather be with Liza. Nadia would like to live alone, so it is all right with her if you want to leave, Russell." They separated that very day, each of them pleased that they were getting what they wanted, yet each of them displeased with me for having told them.

Del and Marlene

I recently attended the wedding of Del and Marlene, young adults whom I have known for about three years. The groom's parents were divorced and both had remarried. Both of Del's parents and stepparents were present, as were Del's maternal and paternal grandparents. His stepmother was the hostess and the official photographer. His stepfather, a minister, performed the ceremony. The bride's mother had been married four times. She and two of her previous husbands were in attendance. She and her second husband gave away the bride. Also present were the bride's paternal grandparents, and the maternal grandfather, and the parents of the first stepfather. The bride has always maintained a close relationship with her "dad," her first stepfather, and, her birth father's parents always include him and his wife in their family gatherings. Together the grandparents, the first stepfather, and the mother provide a secure, dependable support system for the young woman.

In many ways, divorce is the test of the Christian counselor. For most of us, helping our friends and loved ones deal with the consequences of troubled and disrupted marriages will be the most difficult challenges we face.

How should the Christian counselor regard divorce? If we were to take Jesus literally, divorce would not be allowed by Christians except on grounds of adultery. As he taught:

> And it was said: "Whoever dismisses his wife, let him give her a divorce certificate." But I tell you that everyone who dismisses his wife other than for fornication makes her commit adultery, and whoever marries a divorced woman commits adultery (Matt. 5:31-32 LDS).

Divorce, if we understand Jesus correctly, is a repudiation of God's original intention that a man and a woman should live together for a lifetime. In his words:

Because of your hardheartedness he wrote you this commandment. But from the beginning of creation male and female he made them; for the sake of this a man should leave his father and mother, and the two shall be one flesh. What God yoked together let not man separate (Mark 10:5-9 LDS).

It is easy to quote the words of Jesus on the subject and wash our hands of those facing marital difficulties. Perhaps our Lord's teaching on divorce was an example of the hyperbole and irony that characterized his teaching. Perhaps he no more meant that divorce should not be permitted than he literally meant that people should cut off their feet or pluck out their eyes, or that his disciples should hate their parents, spouses, and siblings. He also said the following:

So if your right eye causes you to stumble, pluck it out and throw it away from you; for it is better for you that one of your members die and not all of your body be thrown on the garbage heap. And if your right hand causes you to stumble, cut it off and throw it away from you; for it is better for you that one of your members die and not all of your body go away on the garbage heap (Matt. 5:29-30 LDS).

Now if your hand or foot scandalizes you, cut it off and throw it away; it is better to enter into life maimed or lame than having two hands or two feet to be thrown into the fire of the ages. And if your eye scandalizes you, pluck it out and throw it away; for it is better to enter into life one-eyed than having two eyes to be cast into the burning garbage heap (Matt. 18:8-9 LDS).

If anyone comes to me and does not hate his father and mother and wife and children and brothers and sisters,

and even his very own life, he cannot be my disciple
(Luke 14:26 LDS).

Divorce is many things. It is the breaking of a
contract, a rejection of responsibility, the declaration
that where there was love there is love no longer.
Divorce is not only the end of a marriage; it is the
dissolution of a family.

In a perfect world, there would be no life-threatening
illness and no divorce. In the real world, there is an
abundance of both. Half of all marriages end in divorce,
including the marriages of conscientious Christians.
For better and worse, marriage for as long "as we both
shall *live*" has been replaced with marriage for "as long
as we both shall *love*." Divorce has become an
unavoidable tragedy.

People would not get divorced for such trivial reasons
if they did not get married for such trivial reasons.
Because we are comfortable with each other, enjoy each
other's company, are sexually attracted to each other
for relatively short periods of time, we make promises
of lifelong fidelity that are more often broken than
kept. Obviously we do not know each other well
enough, expect too much of each other, are not
sufficiently prepared for changed circumstances, and
cannot honor our commitments.

No one has to marry, any more than any one has to
have sex. We marry for love. Or do we?

The love for which we marry is a euphoric, ecstatic,
blissful state—a kind of egotism for two. Like all intense
states, the bliss fades. If we are fortunate, it endures for
a few months, waxes and wanes for a few years, and is
replaced by something more secure, comfortable, and
lasting. The honeymoon gives way to companionship,
emotional and sexual intimacy, and a stable environment for rearing children.

Married love (as opposed to romantic love) is not a gush of emotions that exhausts itself when the feelings change. It is both a gift and a hard-won achievement. There is no way that some marriages can succeed. Any objective third party can see that. The lovers have nothing in common, have too much going against them, are too inexperienced, have the burden of past failures and interfering in-laws. Most of the time, the objective third parties are right. But having perfectly adjusted personalities, adequate income, the sexual proclivities of satyrs, loving relatives, *et al,* cannot guarantee that a marriage will work.

Romantic love is based on the assumption that an individual can overcome self-dissatisfaction by joining his or her limited self to another limited self. The two become a new entity. He projects on her the fulfillment of his inadequacies, and she projects on him the fulfillment of hers. Each of the lovers feels freed of the burdens of past failures and personal deficiencies, and they believe both individually and together that the beloved has removed the emptiness, loneliness, and despair of the past.

Such love is a feeling, second only to fear of death in intensity. It can change one's appearance, quicken the senses, transform the most human life into a phantasm of excitement, accentuate one's sense of self-worth, evoke the tenderest of feelings in the hardest of hearts.

Romantic love is only a feeling, and like all feelings, its reign over the affairs of the individual is short. To marry in order to find fulfillment or in the belief that the ecstatic feelings can be maintained indefinitely is to place one's marriage under a death sentence. The illusion of total mutual self-fulfillment has little future. No person can perfect and complete another. When the ecstatic feelings have been used up, the individual is left

where he or she began—with the difficult job of
self-discovery and self-fulfillment.

I am I and you are you. We are not a new continent
but two separate islands, after all. That's the way things
are. There is no need for this realization to be regarded
as a tragedy unless one or both of the lovers cannot
accept the reality of the situation. If they can accept
responsibility, there is a basis for renegotiating the
marriage contract, for transforming the momentary
bliss of romance into the enduring partnership of a
family life.

*No person has it in his or her power to make another person
happy.* If either cannot accept this fact, he or she will
look for someone new on whom to project the desired
traits. By falling out of love with one's first beloved and
into love with a new object of adoration, the self-
dissatisfied individual repeats the error of all romantic
love. No person can heal and transform another. Only
God can.

I am not arguing that we should leave our spouses
and move into the nearest monastery or convent. What
I am saying is that people would not get divorced for the
wrong reasons if they did not get married for the wrong
reasons. We expect too much of marriage and of our
partners, but too little of ourselves. A good marriage is a
work of art, a creation, like a painting or a novel or a
sculpture. Artistic creativity requires talent, expertise,
virtuosity, mentors, and hard work. Why should a
creative marriage require less? It was Michelangelo's
skill, training, and discipline that made him a great
artist. He was also blessed with opportunities, recognition, and financial support. For a marriage to work
there must be similar elements. Each party must have
the ability to communicate, compromise, and change.
Each must be concerned with the other's opportunities.
Each must recognize, appreciate, and respect the

other's distinctiveness, and each must be willing to openly confront the unavoidable issues—time, money, sex, values, religion, family. There should be examples of good marriages that each wants to emulate (or of bad marriages that each wants to avoid). There must be a capacity for self-examination, self-criticism, and adjustment. Even all of these cannot guarantee success. At some point, there must be a deliberate commitment to making the marriage work—a surrender to the other, a transcending of self-centeredness, and a recognition that there is a basis for marriage even more fundmental than the quest for self-satisfaction—marriage as the inception of a family.

Long before the coming of ethical monotheism, society condoned, encouraged, and promoted marriage as the very building block of civilization. Through marriage the male urge to dominate, control, and enjoy a succession of females is sublimated to the male's desire to build for the future, to pass his name and accomplishments on to the next generation, and to enjoy here and now a reassuring sense of permanence. The female's need for protection during pregnancy and through her child-rearing years is satisfied, and her role as nurturer is enhanced. The basic need of both sexes for lifelong relationships that establish the boundaries of one's life, and the functions and purposes of one's existence are provided. Children's needs not only for sustenance, shelter, clothing, comfort, and love but for role models and guides are met. And the comforts of home and hearth are established—there is someplace to go when no one else wants us; there is someone who cares and will help when no one else gives a damn. In old age, there is someone to care about, and, if need be, care for those to whom self-satisfaction and erotic pleasure are only memories. To be sure, this is the way marriage ought to be; not the way it always is. Society depends on permanent marriages and stable families and, when it acts in its own interest, supports both. For clearly all that weakens family is a sin against the common good.

If this is the way marriage and family ought to be, why are they not this way? In our own time, we actively foster the disintegration of marriage and the family even as we nostalgically sing the praises of earlier times, when children respected their elders and most marriages endured. (Why are there no more great TV series about ideal old-fashioned families such as "The Waltons" and "I Remember Mama"? Clearly, nostalgia is not what it used to be!) As a nation, we give lip service to the idea of an enduring family, but we have no public commitment to family survival. There are no pensions for women who leave the job force to raise children, no adequate federal subsidies for day care centers, no incentives to big business to grant maternity leave or provide nursery facilities on the premises. Our welfare policy fosters generation after generation of impoverished, one-parent families.

We have systematically knocked the props out from under traditional images of marriage and family. Economic necessity has chased women out of the home and into the marketplace. A married mother who has neither a job nor a career identifies herself apologetically as "only a housewife." Caring for the needs of the young and instilling values is left to such surrogate parents as babysitters, day care centers, the schools, peers, and the media. The support system previously provided by the extended family is often destroyed by career-required mobility. The occasional long distance phone call and the holiday visit are simply no substitutes for the day-by-day availability of grandparents, aunts, uncles, and cousins.

We have made divorce easy and family survival hard. Television, the movies, and other popular media encourage the sexual curiosity and experimentation of the young while they oppose advertising contraceptives. The result? An epidemic of teenage pregnancies. The single-parent family—a rarity a few decades ago—is as common today as the two-parent family. Unwed mothers and formerly wed mothers, many of them fallen from middle-class existence to poverty, swell the welfare rolls. Such mothers are excluded from educational and career opportunities and are hard pressed to provide for their families' needs.

And steadily increasing is the number of no-parent families. I counsel many upper middle-class families in which a girl of fourteen or fifteen bears a child, turns responsibility for the infant over to her less than enthusiastic mother, and returns to her high school activities. The grandmother, usually a woman in her late thirties with interests and career plans of her own, puts her life on hold and pays the inevitable price. She becomes resentful and depressed. What of the children for whom no one accepts responsibility? They are case studies in insecurity, negative self-image, and antisocial resentment. Life had sent them out as sheep among the wolves.

Typically, a young person is driven by the strongest sexual urges at an age when he or she has no particular economic value, is given little responsibility, and is emotionally unprepared to assume it. Not yet adults and no longer children, adolescents occupy a twilight zone, concerned mostly with immediate gratification, peer approval, and conspicuous consumption. (The shopping mall has replaced the malt shop as the place to hang out and be seen.) Our society surrounds them with temptations and allows them to earn just enough money to pay for nonessentials. Their expectations overstimulated by advertising, they defend themselves against boredom and their inability to communicate through the immediate excitement of sex, drugs, rock music, and speed. When their universe becomes too chaotic, painful, and confusing, appalling numbers kill themselves.

What is the most destructive force to family stability in America? The American family itself. For three decades, our society has been involved in a revolution in its understanding of the meaning, functions, and responsibilities of the family. During this revolution we remain thoroughly confused about male and female roles, children's need and rights, obligations to the elderly.

I have counseled hundreds of parents who accused some outside force (e.g., cults, drugs, boy friends or girl friends, society, the schools, sexual mores) of destroying their families. When we had sorted through the wreckage, we found that many of these families had self-destructed as healthy organisms long before the external threat had presented itself. The parents had been caught up in the need to earn, to have, to get more, to preserve what they had, and to ensure that their children had the same opportunities. In the process something precious had died. The family—that for which the parents had undertaken their harrowing, demanding way of life—had, for all purposes, ceased to function; for there was little time or energy left for listening, communicating, sharing, and caring.

Making a marriage work today in our society is a hard job. Being a family is even harder. Few of us have the talent, dedication, or discipline to accept unconditional responsibility for our own lives, our marriages, and our families, so we find outside influences to blame while we numb ourselves with ceaseless activity and our favorite drugs (television, alcohol, sexual escapades, religion, and gadgets).

The Christian concept of marriage incorporates two incompatible demands: (1) the commitment of a man and a woman in marriage should be for life; their priorities should be each other's satisfaction and fulfillment and the creation of a family and (2) as important as such commitments are, a vow for life may be impossible. We are sinful human beings, and we fail. The job of the Christian as counselor is twofold: (1) to encourage the commitment to marriage and the family and (2) when marriages fail and families disintegrate, to serve as instruments of God's peace and love.

The rules of the Christian counselor who deals with troubled marriages and divorce may be summarized as follows:

1. *Never encourage a marriage to fail.* A good marriage lasts for fifty years; a divorce is for ever. There is enough in our society that pulls families apart—careerism, materialism, distance from supportive parents and friends, change, failure to communicate, and tension between generations. Don't add to it.

2. *Never take sides, even if one of the parties is your friend and the other is not.* It is poor strategy. It tends to increase the tensions of the situation, and it can backfire. Let's imagine that your best friend Suzy complains to you for the hundredth time about her husband Ken's bad temper. You tell her not to put up with it anymore. Should Ken and Suzy get back together, Ken will not appreciate the fact that you sided with Suzy; and Suzy will be too embarrassed to speak to you again. If they do not get back together, one or both of them will hold you responsible. Either way, you will have lost your friends. As it says in Proverbs: "He who meddles in a quarrel not his own is like one who takes a passing dog by the ears" (26:17).

Your role should be a sounding board, reconciler, and mediator—but never judge and jury. Give no advice unless you are asked and only if your relationship is well established and secure.

3. *Teach lovers to be friends.* Try to balance the notion of marriage for mutual self-satisfaction with the concept of marriage as a commitment to each other, as the building of a family, and as a creation.

4. *When dealing with sexual difficulties, remember that sex is mostly in the head; not in the bed.* Sexual gratification requires an environment of trust, intimacy, and communication. It is a precarious balancing between giving and receiving, between being in control and surrendering control to another. Like marriage itself, sexual compatibility is a process of creation, requiring patience, experimentation, and relaxation. When you hear complaints from one party of not getting, suggest more giving. When you hear complaints that the other party is growing distant and disinterested, suggest aggressive and deliberate action. Often the party who complains the most is the one who is investing the least time, caring, and sharing of self.

Sexual pleasure for its own sake is a vicious cycle. There is no such thing as enough pleasure. Yesterday's ecstatic highs are today's routine tedium. It is the mutual self-respect, sharing of significant experiences, and enjoyment of the other that add the coloration and flavor to a relationship and convert passion into intimacy. In the long run, liking is as important as loving.

If pleasure is all that your friend wants, suggest masturbation. After all, self-gratification is safe, intense, and uncomplicated. It is restricted only by the imagination. Real sex is limited by inhibitions, awkwardness, shame, shyness, reticence, inexperience, and mismatched expectations.

5. *When dealing with money problems, remember that basic human needs are equivalent to 120 percent of income.* The more money persons have, the more they need. The more they earn, the larger their deficit.

Also be aware that people are more secretive and deceptive about money than about their sex lives. They either don't want to talk about it or they are so concerned with appearance that they lie. Yet disagreements about money and tensions caused by unpaid bills probably cause more marital discord than arguments about in-laws, children, or watching seventeen football bowl games between Christmas and New Year's Day.

If you are asked for advice, suggest the following:

(a) Plastic surgery—cut up your credit cards and live on cash. If you can't afford something, don't buy it.

(b) Budget and review—to overcome the out-of-control feeling about your finances, prepare a detailed list of your projected income and expenses for the next month, the next quarter, the next year. Review your actual income and expenses at monthly intervals, analyze waste and overspending, and revise your budget as needed.

(c) If possible, pay bills promptly—don't squirrel away bills until the end of the month. It is too easy to spend the money on other things and end up behind the eight ball.

(d) Pay yourself first—put at least 5 percent of your income into an individual retirement fund or a savings account. If you lack the resolve to do this, arrange to have the money automatically withdrawn from your paycheck or checking account.

(e) Get the generosity habit—contribute at least 5 percent of your income to your church, your favorite cause, and others in need and expect nothing in return.

Money is power. The more we spend on ourselves and our own "needs," the less powerful we become. The more we concern ourselves with others and bestow our power on them, the more power we have. Generosity is good for you; generous people are happy people. They have overcome the misery and anxiety of self-absorption. They are a delight to themselves and others. Acts of kindness are remembered and their consequences remain long after the most eloquent speech, the most orthodox theology, and the most difficult achievement have been completely forgotten.

(f) Stop playing money's victim; start being its student. Subscribe to a personal money management magazine; spend a day a month in the finance section of your library; seek the advice of those whom you respect. I am not suggesting the pursuit of get-rich-quick schemes, but educating oneself in the basics of spending, saving, and investing. Most of the people I know act as if they are idiots when it comes to mortgages, mutual funds, and life insurance. They seem to think that what they don't know can't hurt them. Wrong!

6. *Find out what the real problem is.* Then find out what the real problem behind the real problem is. Are your friends arguing about money, or sex, or their children's hair style, when the real issue is control? Is your friend Cliff complaining about his wife Nancy's housekeeping and cooking, when his problem is really his guilt about an extramarital affair? Is Jane moaning about being treated by her husband and children as their full-time maid, chauffeur, and tour director while at the same time she is insisting that they should always rely on her? Try to find out what is at stake, and if possible, to mediate the differences.

7. *If divorce occurs, help the divorced persons deal with*

their grief-reaction with its attendant denial, anger, bargaining, and related responses. Frequently one party in a divorce acts as though the whole thing is not really happening and passively waits for the other party to return. The sooner your friend accepts what is happening and gets on with his or her life, the better. Urge your friend to balance the following: (a) learning the lessons of past failures, (b) reassessing who he or she really is; and (c) planning for a hopeful future. Inevitably, the recently divorced person will get stuck in self-pity or rage. A good friend should help break the emotional logjam. (See suggestions for loss counseling in chapter 14.)

8. *Help your friend's children deal with their feelings—fear, loss, self-blame, confusion, and divided loyalty.* A supportive adult who is not part of the disintegrating family can provide compassion, sympathy, and an objective point of view. Children are deeply hurt by divorce. They tend to blame themselves, take on themselves the impossible responsibility for reconciling their parents, and feel abandoned and humilitated. They have little comprehension of the real issues that set one adult against the other, and frequently cannot even articulate the pain they feel, so listen carefully to what they say and do not say. Draw them out whenever possible and help them gain perspective. But most important, provide them with a safety zone where they are unconditionally accepted.

9. *Help the stepparents deal with the most impossible job in the world.* Most divorced persons remarry. If there are children from the first marriage, the new spouse finds a ready-made family, but like clothes bought off the rack, the fit is far from perfect. Being a stepmother or stepfather is probably the most difficult role that an individual can assume. In the midst of making all the adjustments that marriage requires, the stepparent is

suddenly immersed in conflicts over authority, finances, visitation, the rights of former in-laws. Popular
mythology paints stepmothers as evil and stepfathers as
abusive and insensitive. (Have you ever read a fairy tale
about *an innocent stepmother* who is exploited by her *evil
stepchildren?*) The stepparent is expected to accept the
full responsibilities of parenting on a day-to-day basis
without any clearly stated rights. The decisions of
stepparents are subject to review by the actual parents,
grandparents, and stepchildren themselves. For the
children of the earlier marriage may resent and taunt
the stepparent, challenging his or her authority at every
turn. Or stepchildren may try to undermine the new
relationships, in the unrealistic expectation that mother
and father will get back together. When there are
children from the stepparent's earlier marriage or
children from the new union, the stresses and strains
can become virtually unbearable. Stepparenting is the
stuff of which film comedies are made, but its demands
and frustrations are far from amusing in actuality.

As a counselor and friend, give your attention,
sympathy, and emotional support to stepparents.

C H A P T E R   17

Responding to Loss of Faith

Case Notes: Louise

Louise, a client of mine, is an embittered thirty-six-year-old ex-nun who, after eighteen years renounced her order. She had been repeatedly disciplined by a superior whose lesbian overtures she had spurned. Now she is painfully enduring the decision making that one customarily associates with adolescence—how to dress, what to do for a living, where to live, whether to have sex on a first date (or at all), what to believe.

Martin

Martin was the minister who assisted at my ordination in 1960. Years later he would turn up as my graduate student. His real love throughout his youth and into adulthood had been aviation. According to the values of his strict upbringing, dedication to the gospel allowed no room for "worldly" pursuits, so he had "taken up his cross" and sacrificed flying. (Despite a profound sense of guilt, he was taking solo instruction on the sly.) Fifteen years of self-denial and "living for others" had scarcely proved fulfilling. His sense of vocation was fading, and it was too late for a career as a pilot. Perhaps, he reasoned, a doctorate in religion would be his ticket to a new start.

Mel

Mel was a convert to a new religious movement—one that the newspapers constantly refer to as a "brainwashing cult." He prospered in the group, held several important posts, and earned a degree from a major university. His parents, who felt that he was wasting his life, had him kidnapped and deprogrammed. For the past seven years he has worked as a deprogrammer himself. He is totally devoted to persuading members of his former group that they are brainwashed and that the group is evil.

Diane

Diane is in her middle thirties, a bright, engaging person, eager to please, quick to smile, pleasant, and open. When I first met her, she had just run away from an ultrafundamentalist sect in the Arizona desert. She was self-conscious, tense, and frightened. She was suffering tremendous ambivalence about seeing me for counseling, a fear that by talking to me in order to alleviate her own anxieties she was betraying the group she had left and, thus, was betraying God. She was afraid that God would punish her, that she would be killed for her failure to submit to his will.

Losing faith is not simply a matter of letting one's church membership lapse or changing one's theological assumptions. For many people, losing faith is life-threatening. For, as we have noted, it is lack or loss of a sense of transcendental mooring that predisposes human beings to the most virulent attacks of anxiety and depression.

For many years, I have studied religious conversions and those who fall away after such conversions. I have noted, for example, that most of the converts to revivalistic Christianity and religious cults drift away within a year. Loss of faith is not limited to recent converts. One of the most intriguing aspects of the years that I spent as a teacher in a university graduate program in religious studies was the large number of mature adults who were using the pursuit of an academic degree as a means of transition from one religious identity to another. Many of my students ranged in age from forty to sixty-five. Some had enjoyed years of success as ministers, priests, nuns, religious educators, or ecclesiastical administrators before returning to school. In most cases, the motivation was more than the quest for additional instruction. They were in the midst of a life crisis. The faith that had once sustained them, the sense of vocation that had brought them satisfaction, and the enthusiasm that had made the struggles of a religious calling worthwhile— all these were disintegrating.

I witnessed with sadness the slipping away of belief, the erosion of authority, the loss of purpose in the lives of many once-stalwart disciples. "I can no longer accept . . . " each of them seemed to be saying. Their idealism was unabated, but their capacity for finding means of expressing that idealism has suddenly dimmed. They had lost faith, and so have those who walk away from today's innovative religious groups, who drop out of the new authoritarian communities, or who simply find that they can no longer believe what they had taken for granted as members of local, denominational churches.

What are the emotional consequences of losing faith? Reactions include confusion, doubt, guilt, anxiety, ambivalence, and lack of direction. In sum, a loss of inner balance characterizes the former believer. Losing faith requires a leap no less drastic than finding it. Whether the act of disavowal stems from a sudden disenchantment or from a gradual waning of loyalty, loss of faith may leave the individual embittered, humiliated, lacking in self-confidence, angry, and depressed. Disavowal triggers grieving reactions similar to those that follow divorce, the death of a family member, a change of vocation, or the end of a love affair.

Many former believers I have interviewed report a mixed reaction of righteousness indignation mingled with fear of having committed a fatal personal error. On the one hand, the former believer feels that he or she has been deluded, manipulated, and exploited by the church or sect an its leadership. On the other hand, the rebel expresses an anxiousness approaching panic: "Perhaps I am making a terrible mistake. God may be trying my faith. Satan may be tempting me. What have I done?"

A common solution is a temporary compromise, living in a no-man's land in which the doctrinal content of the deserted church or sect is still affirmed by the individual while the leadership or members of the group are rejected as hypocrites, traitors, heretics who have betrayed the "true faith." Those who defect from the group because of their perception that the group has betrayed its own ideals may attempt to survive in reformed cells numbering from a handful to a righteous remnant of one or two. Since the righteous remnant is not as thoroughly disoriented as the utterly disenchanted, the loss of identity with its accompanying ennui, self-alienation, and confusion is less pronounced.

More typical is a former Moonie whom I have tracked from the day he first encountered the recruiters of the Unification Church, through his conversion and career among the faithful, through his disenchantment, departure, and disavowal of the church, until his present life in a locale and a life-style far removed from his days as a follower of Reverend Sun Myung Moon. Today he respects the Moonies, despises the Moonies, fears the Moonies, and belittles the Moonies. His defection is irrevocable and unconditional but his utterances concerning the sect are irreconcilable. To admit total self-deception, to characterize the sect as solely evil, is to view oneself in a most negative manner—as a weak-willed dupe, a fool, a pawn. To grant too much value to the sect and its way of life is to raise the possibility that defection signifies grievous error, self-betrayal, or sloth. Hence, ambivalence is the best defense and the most comfortable psychological habitation.

Losing faith is like falling out of love. The rapturous sense of oneness disappears. The individual's feeling of isolation returns. The attachment to the beloved that enabled the lover to escape the finitude of a solitary ego has been sundered. "I am I, and you are you, and we shall remain divided." The convert finds himself alone and less than totally perfected and is anchored by circumstances and responsibilities to a mundane world that stubbornly refuses to disappear or accept redemption. Life is again difficult, awkward, and painful.

When faith no longer works, former zealots have several choices:

(a) They may shrug their shoulders, accept the "benefits" gained from their time with the group, and return to their former life.

(b) They may counter-convert, that is compensate for disappointed expectations by loving what they formerly shunned and hating what they previously adored.

(c) The disappointed believers may find a worthier object of their total devotion. Former believers are particularly vulnerable to romantic involvements, holy causes, and heroes. Many of the pre–Jonestown defectors from the People's Temple were devotees of self-proclaimed psychic advisers or fundamentalist Christian sects when I first met them. Nature abhors a vacuum; when faith is lost, some new dependence is likely to rush in to take its place.

(d) The individuals may become cynical, hiding their true feelings behind a wall of irony, humor, and sarcasm.

(e) They may interpret their release from the group as the beginning of a period of creative freedom and boundless self-realization.

Counseling those who have lost faith requires patience and compassion. This is true whether they have left a demanding group to which they have at one time converted or have simply found that they can no longer find meaning in the faith that they have unquestioningly pursued since birth. The counselor must not take the former believer's problem as an attack on the counselor's faith or as an opportunity to win a convert to the counselor's group or beliefs. Accept former believers as they are and where they are. If they have spurned their former faith and walked away, give them the opportunity to tell their story. At the proper point, you may be able to help them distinguish between their former faith and their former associates. There are no perfect churches. If there were, you and I would be banned from entering their doors lest we contaminate them.

The most common form of counter-conversion is the acceptance of what I term a "perverse life-style." Former believers act as though they could get even with whatever disappointed them in the past by loving what they formerly spurned and spurning what they formerly loved. There seems to be as many former puritans who have become libertines as there are former libertines who have become puritans. Ultimately counter-conversion is compulsive and unsatisfying. Ask your friends if they are any freer today rebelling against their former way of life than they were when they followed it. Who is pulling their chain?

Beware of conversion careers. Some of our friends will appear to have a new identity—new beliefs, values, attitudes, patterns of behavior, and rules for child rearing—every six months. Tactfully remind them of their history, indicate your skepticism, and ask them what they are really looking for. It is perfectly all right for you to tell someone you care for, "Come on, Dorothy. It's time for you to click your heels together, say, 'there's no place like home,' and return to Kansas." Your friend may get angry. But counselors, like parents, have to set some limits. An individual who sloughs off identities like a snake shedding skins is en route to big trouble. Having no fixed identity is as destructive to relationships, marriage, family, and one's well-being as having an inflexible and judgmental disposition. (The two most difficult types to counsel are those with no sense of humor and those to whom everything is a joke.)

If you see your friends go from religious zealotry to romantic attachment, or from romantic attachment to religious zealotry, try to relate to them the nature of the dependence-rescue-resentment cycle. The more difficulty a person has accepting responsibility for his or her own life, the more likely he or she is to become an addictive personality. As a counselor, you do not want to rescue and make your friends dependent on you. You want to make them aware of the pattern their life exhibits.

It may sound self-contradictory, but take sarcasm

seriously. For behind it lurks enormous pain, depression, and self-destructiveness. The cynical wit of the ex-believer can be most amusing, but it is ultimately gallows humor. Respond to sarcastic or cynical friends as you would to any morose persons. I am not saying that cynics are more likely to commit suicide than others. That is not true. The people most at risk are the ones who cannot communicate their pain at all. What is self-destructive about sarcastic persons is that they build walls against what they most want—the love of others and self-respect. Ordinary people soon tire of them; other cynics resent them because they are competing for attention; and the cynics are left with what they least want—their own company.

How should the Christian counselor deal with cynics? Tell them to knock it off. Ask them where it hurts, and give them a hug.

If your friends feel freed by their rejection of what they once believed, afford them the opportunity to do what they claim they are doing. Let their lives bloom before you. Give them every chance to impress you with what they become, but get even with them. Let your life so shine before them that they are dazzled. Tell your story. Express your doubts and the way you have resolved them. If they are unresolved, share that too. Doubt is not the enemy of faith. Fear is. Stop making a secret of what you believe and what you are living for. Without apology or equivocation, be who you are.

CONCLUSION

Until Christmas

As I write these words, Christmas is almost upon me. There are only a few days left for me to think about how best to regather our scattered family, to worry about giving and getting, to sort out any accumulated holiday hurts, and to deal with my well-earned weariness. I am looking forward to the Christmas Eve Eucharist at our small church, to those few quiet minutes for contemplating the mystery of our faith. I believe that this observance of the Eucharist only minutes before the day that celebrates the birth of King Jesus is at once the most sublime and paradoxical act that can ever be performed. For by our sharing of the Lord's Supper, we are uniting our joy and gratitude for the coming of the true King with our sorrow and repentance that he must suffer and die for each of us.

With God all things are possible. For God is the almighty, all-knowing, everlasting, ruler of the universe. His power and knowledge are limitless. Until the coming of the Christ. Until the birth of his Son. Until the sovereign Lord of Creation surrenders himself to the state and fate of humankind. From the very moment that the Christ child is born, God lays aside his omnipotence and places the fulfillment of his purpose in our hands. The initiative remains God's, but by our response we may accomplish or frustrate the divine plan for our lives, our loved ones, our society, or our world.

Many years ago when I was a teenager, some friends and I were in the observation tower of the then tallest structure in Chicago, the Prudential Building. As we peered down at the automobiles shrunken by the distance to the size of toys and the pedestrians to the dimension of scurrying ants, the most religious of my companions remarked, "This must be how we look to God." His innocent words expressed a sense of childlike awe and wonder, but they also ignored the message of Christmas. God is no emperor of an intergalactic federation who monitors us with refined instruments of scientific scrutiny. He is with us now and for all time—closer to each of us than we are to ourselves. God is present in the life of each Christian, striving to perfect you and me in love, luring us into the discovery of what we can be, seducing us, tricking us into sharing, caring, loving, and being loved.

Most of the time, we do not respond to one another as human beings but as categories. I put you into some hard and fast category and respond not to you but to my own mental construct about you. You may do the same to me. When I am introduced to a stranger, I may be asked, "What is it that you do?" And whatever I reply becomes the basis for 90 percent of all the thoughts or feelings the stranger will ever entertain toward me. If I say I am a minister, he or she will be careful not to tell off-color jokes in my presence, apologize for having missed church last Sunday, and be sure that I am not invited to the next cocktail party. If I say I am retired, the stranger would want to know "retired from what"? so that he or she would be able to pigeonhole who I was and what I was like as a person. If the stranger could not comfortably work me into a preestablished category, he or she would always feel unsettled in my presence.

The Chinese have a saying they use to explain prejudice and hatred toward others, "Call a dog a bad name and shoot it." Once you have categorized someone, you are no longer responsible to treat that person as a human being. We characterize our enemies as insects, animals, or things and then feel justified to exploit them or take their lives. When someone disagrees with us or acts in a manner of which we do not approve, we declare that person "sick" or "crazy" or "brainwashed." From that point on we can react to the label and pay no attention to the reality of the person. But the ministry and example of the Christ challenges every assumption as to who is good and who is evil, who is worthy of our caring and who is not. Jesus enjoyed the company of the most despised of his people. That does not mean that he spurned such conventionally upright individuals as Nicodemus and Joseph of Arimathea. Jesus knew men and women of every class and condition, knew them inside and out, and was impressed not by their titles, stations, and positions, but only by who they were.

The lesson to be learned is that when I respond to you and you respond to me without prejudice and preconception, we are both changed. We know and are united with each other. We know and are restored to ourselves. Where any life touches another life deeply, each person is able to be who he or she is and be responded to as who he or she is. And when to you I become a real flesh-and-blood person and not just the categories in which you place me, you will find out who you are and reveal it. And when I respond fully to you, I will find out who I am and reveal it. As we noted earlier, through such openness and only through such openness can the healing, teaching, reforming, and redeeming of persons be accomplished. To paraphrase the apostle John, don't tell me that you love God, show me by loving me (I John 4:19-21).

If you and I want to hear the voice of God, it is time for us to start listening to one another. We must forget everything we think we know about one another and allow ourselves to feel the loneliness, the pain, the fullness, the joy of our brothers and sisters. Only if we ignore the categories, the shallow psychologizing about one another, can we discern the willingness to share, to serve, to love (as well as the hunger for sharing, serving, and being loved) that fills us like a cloud of incense whenever two or three of us are gathered together.

The test of a religion is not the degree of its theological development or the beauty of its worship or the intensity of its devotional life, but the sensitivity of its adherents to the needs of other human beings—to the needs of the stranger next door, the friend in the next pew or at the next shop bench, the lonely, the confused, the hungry, the sick. How does one acquire this sensitivity? By the simple and yet profound act of accepting the gift now and always offered—the living God who stands ready to plunge himself into our lives, to bless and enhance the highest highs and the deepest lows or our existence so that in, through, and despite us, the miracle of Christmas, the sacrifice of Good Friday, and the promise of Easter may daily be renewed.

For, to paraphrase Meister Eckhart, if the Christ is born in Bethlehem a million times and trudges the dusty roads of Palestine, preaching for a million years, but is not born in your heart and life—and in my heart and life—then what difference does his gospel make? But if you and I are crucified with the Christ and yet we live because he lives in us, then the good news is true: *God is for us. God is with us. God is in us. God is among us. And we are thankful.*